Turkey's New Foreign Policy
Davutoglu, the AKP and the Pursuit of Regional Order

Aaron Stein

www.rusi.org

Royal United Services Institute for Defence and Security Studies

Turkey's New Foreign Policy: Davutoglu, the AKP and the Pursuit of Regional Order
Aaron Stein
First published 2014

Whitehall Papers series

Series Editor: Professor Malcolm Chalmers
Editors: Adrian Johnson, Ashlee Godwin and Cathy Haenlein

RUSI is a Registered Charity (No. 210639)
ISBN 978-1-138-90723-2

Published on behalf of the Royal United Services Institute for Defence
and Security Studies
by
Routledge Journals, an imprint of Taylor & Francis, 4 Park Square,
Milton Park, Abingdon OX14 4RN

SUBSCRIPTIONS
Please send subscription orders to:

USA/Canada: Taylor & Francis Inc., Journals Department, 530 Walnut Street, Suite 850, Philadelphia, PA 19106, USA

UK/Rest of World: Routledge Journals, T&F Customer Services, T&F Informa UK Ltd, Sheepen Place, Colchester, Essex CO3 3LP, UK

Contents

About the Author

Aaron Stein is an Associate Fellow of RUSI and a PhD Candidate at King's College London, where he is researching Iranian and Turkish nuclear decision-making. He holds a BA in Political Science from the University of San Francisco and a Master's degree in International Policy Studies with a specialisation in nuclear non-proliferation from the Monterey Institute of International Studies.

He has written extensively on Turkish politics and regional proliferation, publishing in scholarly journals and print media, including *Survival*, the *RUSI Journal*, the *New York Times*, *Foreign Affairs*, *Foreign Policy*, the *Bulletin of Atomic Scientists* and the *National Interest*.

Acknowledgements

I am extremely grateful to all those who supported me in the writing of this Whitehall Paper. I began my research while living in Turkey and benefited extensively from conversation with academics, former government officials and other policy analysts about Turkish foreign policy. These conversations provided the essential foundations of this work.

I would particularly like to thank Jonathan Eyal, who first approached me about writing for RUSI in November 2011 and has since become a mentor. Along the way, Behlul Ozkan, Hugh Pope, Henri Barkey and Michael Stephens were particularly forthcoming with their time and expertise. Shashank Joshi and Dov Friedman were similarly helpful and provided advice and comments at numerous different stages of this project. Malcolm Chalmers was also exceptionally generous and the paper benefited considerably from his insightful comments on each draft. The paper was helped tremendously by the patient and expert editing of Adrian Johnson, Ashlee Godwin, Cathy Haenlein and Amitha Rajan. Without their efforts, the final product would have been of lesser quality and much more difficult to read.

Many other individuals provided feedback, whether in writing or in conversation. Some of these wish to remain anonymous, but I would particularly like to thank Daniel Dombey, Steven A Cook, Michael Koplow, Hassan Hassan, Mary Fitzgerald and Charles Lister. I am also grateful to others who commented on a draft at a workshop held at RUSI in August 2014; this indispensable feedback enabled me to truly focus my thoughts in writing this paper. Finally, I would like to thank my wife, Seda Savas-Stein, and my family, David, Karol and Matt.

Any errors or shortcomings are, of course, mine alone.

I. INTRODUCTION: THE SEARCH FOR STRATEGIC DEPTH – THE AKP AND THE MIDDLE EAST

Since coming to power in 2002, Turkey's Justice and Development Party (AKP) has sought to play a larger diplomatic role in the Middle East, which had suffered years of neglect by previous governments.

The AKP evolved from Turkey's Islamist political movement,[1] the first iteration of which had begun in 1970, after Necmettin Erbakan established the Milli Nizam Partisi (National Order Party). Over the following years, this movement advocated for closer links to Turkey's Muslim-majority neighbours, and was hampered by frequent party closures in the wake of military coups or as a result of an order by the Constitutional Court.

In the November 2002 election, however, the AKP won 34.2 per cent of the national vote. Although it had emerged as Turkey's most popular party, the AKP nevertheless had to contend with the very real threat of another 'post-modern' coup until 2008, when it survived a closure case put forward by secular elements in Turkey's bureaucracy by one vote.[2]

The AKP emerged from this closure case with its popularity far exceeding that of its closest competitor, the Kemalist Republican People's Party (CHP). The Turkish electorate's support for the AKP was in part simply a reflection of the country's conservative political majority. However, between 2002 and 2010, a large segment of Turkish liberals were also attracted to the AKP and its liberal rhetoric and democratic reforms. These factors gave the AKP a more solid electoral mandate to push forward with its own agenda, free from the bureaucratic restraints that had stifled it before the 2008 closure case.

---

[1] Yildiz Atasoy, *Turkey, Islamists and Democracy: Transition and Globalization in a Muslim State* (New York, NY: I B Tauris, 2005), pp. 81–85.
[2] Robert Tait, 'Turkey's Governing Party Avoids Being Shut Down for Anti-Secularism', *Guardian*, 30 July 2008.

Capitalising on this greater sense of political freedom, from 2009 the party's approach to foreign affairs began to change considerably, with Ahmet Davutoglu – a former professor of international relations who is now the Turkish prime minister – assuming the position of foreign minister in May of that year. Thus, while the AKP's ideology has remained consistent during its time in power, it was only gradually realised as the party's power grew.

Ankara has historically paid close attention to regional developments. However, Turkey's foreign policy in the region since its foundation as a separate state in 1923 was defined by its preference for non-intervention and neutrality in the areas which, until the First World War, had formed part of the Istanbul-centred Ottoman Empire. The AKP government has rejected this approach, choosing instead to adopt a proactive foreign policy aimed at creating 'strategic depth' by expanding Turkey's zone of influence in the Middle East, drawing on the opportunities of geography, economic power and imperial history to reconnect the country with its historical hinterland. Unsurprisingly, this approach has garnered considerable interest from scholars.

This policy is based on the work of Ahmet Davutoglu and it is rooted in the belief that the Eurasian landmass, and the areas that surround it, are of crucial importance to global geopolitics. As such, Turkey, which sits at the centre of this vital piece of land, is deemed to have a unique opportunity to expand its influence and create strategic depth. In doing so, it is held, it can establish itself as a global power and thereby play a significant role in creating new global institutions that are more in keeping with the world's different 'civilisations' or cultures. Thus, breaking from past approaches to foreign policy, this interpretation of geopolitics is based on an assumption that the spread of Western power into the Balkans, Central Asia and the Middle East is incongruent with Turkish national interests and must be reversed.

This Whitehall Paper will outline the key tenets of the AKP's policy of strategic depth, with particular reference to how they apply to the Middle East. The paper will begin with a discussion of the theories that underpin the AKP's foreign policy. It will then discuss how the party's current approach to foreign affairs differs from traditional Turkish foreign policy. Finally, it will show how the theories that underpin strategic depth are reflected in the formulation and implementation of the AKP's current policies towards various countries in the Middle East, as well as assessing how they have shaped Ankara's approach to key regional events, such as the Arab upheavals and the Syrian civil war. Of course, in order to provide a full picture of the implications of this new turn in foreign policy, it would also be necessary to examine Turkey's evolving role in Central Asia and the Balkans, alongside its changing relationships with the US and the EU. However, these dimensions are largely outside the scope of this paper.

This introductory chapter will explore the theoretical underpinnings of the policy of strategic depth. The second chapter will document Turkey's initial efforts to mediate regional conflicts and its policies in relation to the Israel-Palestine question. It will also explore the AKP's policies in Iraq and Syria between 2002 and 2011 – two countries that some in the AKP consider as part of Turkey's 'natural hinterland'. The third chapter will describe the pattern of Turkish policy during the Arab upheavals that began at the end of 2010, as well as Ankara's support for religiously conservative political parties in Egypt, Libya and Tunisia. The final chapter will discuss Turkey's approach to the conflicts in Syria and Iraq since 2011. The paper will conclude with an analysis of the AKP's future policy options and the viability of its current approach to Middle Eastern affairs.

Benign Neglect: Turkey's Historical Approach to the Middle East

As the heir to the Ottoman Empire, Turkey has a long history of involvement in the Middle East. However, following the declaration of the Turkish Republic in 1923, policy-makers adopted a policy of non-intervention in the region. This policy was based on the mantra of the country's first president, Mustafa Kemal Ataturk (1923–38): 'peace at home, peace abroad'. The articulation of this policy came after the dismemberment of the Ottoman Empire by the European powers, as well as the resolution of disputes over Mosul in the 1920s and the incorporation of the province of Hatay into Turkey in 1939. Early Turkish policy-makers instead remained focused on domestic reforms, aimed at advancing the institutions and new national identity of the young Turkish Republic, rather than on regional affairs.

After the end of the Second World War, Turkish foreign policy-makers abandoned their previous preference for neutralism in favour of an alliance with the Western states, primarily due to concerns about the Soviet Union. After the end of the war, Turkey found itself surrounded by the Soviet Union and its proxies, and felt a need to ally itself with a more powerful state to ensure that its territorial integrity was not threatened. To this end, Turkey, as early as 1947, asked the US to grant it a formal security assurance.

After half a decade of lobbying, Turkey joined NATO in 1952 and began to implement a regional policy aimed at halting the spread of communism. In line with this, during the 1950s Ankara worked to limit the spread of Egyptian-inspired pan-Arabism in Soviet-allied Syria and Iraq. These efforts were encouraged by the US, which in the same period sought to use coercive diplomacy to limit the inroads made by the Soviet Union into the Arab world.[3]

After the 1950s, however, Turkish leaders turned their attention away from the Middle East, and instead focused on the threats they faced on their western and eastern borders. Ankara's reasons for doing so were twofold. First, its NATO commitments included the deployment of the bulk of its military along its border with Warsaw Pact countries. Second, NATO was hesitant to support Turkey in an 'out-of-area' war in the Middle East. Indeed, there was concern that the deployment of Turkish forces along its borders with the Middle East would detract from NATO's strength along its southern flank with the Soviet Union, whilst also risking a clash with Soviet-allied forces in Iraq and Syria. The latter scenario could in turn lead to Turkey's invocation of the collective-defence provision, thereby detracting from the defence of Western Europe.[4]

Turkey's broad neglect of the Middle East continued until the early 1980s. In September 1980, the Turkish military dissolved the country's parliament, arrested the leaders of the major political parties, which it abolished, and placed the country under the control of General Kenan Evren. In turn, the military junta gave responsibility for the country's economy to Turgut Ozal, former under-secretary to the prime minister and a former World Bank employee. With the military's backing, Ozal embarked upon a series of reforms intended to transform Turkey's economy from an autarkic, statist system to an export-oriented, capitalist system. In 1983, he was elected prime minister and he pursued these reforms until his death a decade later.

The resulting economic transition led to the growth of Turkey's private industry, which began to seek export markets for its new products. This search eventually led Turkish companies to Ankara's Middle Eastern neighbours to the south. Yet, while the country's economic relations with the Middle East were beginning to develop, the rise of the Kurdistan Workers' Party (PKK) – which initiated an insurgency against the Turkish state in 1984 – prevented any major rapprochement with the leaderships of Iran and Syria, which, at various times, have nurtured close ties with the

---

[3] Peter L Hahn, 'Securing the Middle East: The Eisenhower Doctrine of 1957', *Presidential Studies Quarterly* (Vol. 36, No. 1, Presidential Doctrines, March 2006), pp. 38–47; William Hale, *Turkish Foreign Policy Since 1774*, 3rd edition (London: Routledge, 2013), p. 92; Ara Sanjian, 'The Formulation of the Baghdad Pact', *Middle East Studies* (Vol. 33, No. 2, April 1997), pp. 226–66.

[4] Turkish scholar Mustafa Kibaroglu notes that Ankara adopted 'a policy of "non-involvement" toward the Middle East', so as to assuage its European Allies' concerns that the country's proximity to the Middle East risked involving NATO in an out-of-area war. See Mustafa Kibaroglu, 'Turkey and Israel Strategize', *Middle East Quarterly* (Vol. 9, No. 1, Winter 2002), pp. 61–65.

militant group.[5] More than 40,000 people have died in the thirty-year conflict between the PKK and the Turkish state. Perhaps unsurprisingly, the Kurdish issue has remained a serious impediment to the furthering of Turkey's relations with its two neighbours, thus preventing the deepening of political and economic ties with numerous states in the region.

The Post-Cold War World

The collapse of the Soviet Union had a considerable impact on Turkey's Middle East policy. At the time, Turkish officials were concerned that the elimination of the Soviet threat could lead to the disbanding of NATO. Ankara feared that the multilateral defence organisation would then be replaced by a new military alliance that would include only EU member states and the US, which would thus see Turkey – as a non-EU member – lose its military links to the US as well as being excluded from a new North Atlantic alliance.

These fears proved to be without merit. Nevertheless, they did influence Turkish decision-making in the years immediately after the end of the Cold War. For example, Ankara sought to bolster ties with Washington in order to retain its significance to American policy-makers in the post-Cold War period. This approach also saw Ankara rebrand itself both as a bulwark against 'rogue regimes' in the region and as a critical outpost to defend against asymmetric threats, including those posed by non-state actors.[6]

Ozal's foreign policy during this period was based on a continued belief in the need to maintain close relations with the US and the EU. In line with this, during the 1990s, Turkish policy emphasised the country's shared interests with the West in containing the spread of radical Islam, and in isolating the regimes in Damascus and Tehran. For Turkey, this stemmed from these regimes' support for the PKK, as well as growing concern over the spread of weapons of mass destruction. Moreover, Ankara signalled a level of comfort with Western involvement in the region rooted in its policy assumption that it had overlapping interests with Washington in the Middle East and would thus benefit from a robust

---

[5] Henri Barkey, 'Turkey's Kurdish Dilemma', *Survival: Global Politics and Strategy* (Vol. 35, No. 4, Winter 1993), p. 53.
[6] Cameron S Brown, 'Turkey in the Gulf Wars of 1991 and 2003', *Turkish Studies* (Vol. 8, No. 1, Spring 2007), pp. 86–87; Muhittin Ataman, 'Ozal Leadership and Restructuring of Turkish Ethnic Policy in the 1980s', *Middle Eastern Studies* (Vol. 38, No. 4, October 2000), pp. 128–29; Haldun Cancia and Sevket Serkan Senb, 'Turkish Dilemma after Operation Desert Storm (1990–1991): An Analysis of Negative Consequences', *European Journal of Social Science Research* (Vol. 23, No. 3, September 2010), pp. 279–92.

American presence in its near abroad, and that its support for US policy would enhance Turkish–American relations.

The AKP's recent emphasis on strategic depth, however, has rejected this approach to foreign policy. For Davutoglu, previous Turkish decision-making was flawed because it was based on a shallow interpretation of Turkey's geography and history.[7] Davutoglu's approach to foreign policy derives from his belief in the potency of Islam as a source of communal strength and political legitimacy, as well as his adoption of turn-of-the-century theories of geopolitics. Key among the latter include Halford John Mackinder's 'Heartland Theory', Nicholas J Spykman's 'Rimland Theory', and the works of Karl Haushofer, whose theories on geopolitics are in turn derived from that of Freidrich Ratzel, who put forward the concept of *lebensraum*.[8] This term has negative historical connotations, of course, but Haushofer's understanding of geopolitics is premised on the argument that borders are not static, but are instead 'dynamic' and 'ever changing'.[9]

These scholars divided the world into zones, known as the 'heartland',[10] comprising much of Central Asia, and the 'rimland',[11] which extended from Western Europe through the Arabian Peninsula to Asia. During the Cold War, these areas were under the influence of either the US or the Soviet Union, thereby preventing the expansion of Turkish influence there.

The collapse of the Soviet Union was thus perceived by Davutoglu as an important opportunity for Turkey to extend its sphere of influence into these vitally important areas. In Central Asia, the newly independent states were predominantly Muslim, had access to vital resources, and had historical and cultural links to Turkey. In the rimland, Davutoglu pointed out, eight of the world's sixteen most important waterways were under the control of Muslim-majority states. In Davutoglu's view, therefore, Turkey's connection to these states via their shared religion provided Ankara with the opportunity to expand its power and create strategic depth.

---

[7] Ahmet Davutoglu, 'Turkiye merkez ulke olmali', *Radikal*, 26 February 2004, <http://www.radikal.com.tr/haber.php?haberno=107581>, accessed 8 October 2014; Ahmet Davutoglu, 'Turkiye'yi Markalastiran "Ritmik Diplomasi"', 24 January 2005, *Netpano.com*, <http://www.netpano.com/turkiyeyi-markalastiran-ritmik-diplomasi/>, accessed 8 October 2014.
[8] Behlul Ozkhan, 'Turkey, Davutoglu and the Idea of Pan-Islam', *Survival: Global Politics and Strategy* (Vol. 56, No. 4, August/September 2014), pp. 119–40.
[9] Holger H Herwig, 'Geopolitik: Haushofer, Hitler and Lebensraum', *Journal of Strategic Studies* (Vol. 22, No. 2–3, 1999), pp. 218–41.
[10] Halford John Mackinder, 'The Geographical Pivot of History', *Geographical Journal* (Vol. 23, No. 4, April 1904), pp. 421–37.
[11] Nicholas J Spykman, 'Geography and Foreign Policy', *American Political Science Review* (Vol. 32, No. 1, February 1938), pp. 38–50.

Davutoglu then drew upon the work of Haushofer to explain why Turkey has natural *lebensraum* in both of these regions, which he described as the country's 'natural hinterland'.[12] In this regard, he argued that Turkey was situated at the centre of the Middle East, the Caucasus and the Balkans, thus providing it with a natural hinterland. In turn, Davutoglu postulated, Turkey's historical links to these areas meant that Ankara possessed a unique understanding of the numerous different cultures in the country's near abroad. This understanding, he argued, would allow Turkey to expand into these areas to carve out a zone of influence throughout much of the area once controlled by the Ottoman Empire. Davutoglu later incorporated this worldview into his foreign policy of 'strategic depth', which would come to be known as 'zero problems with neighbours'. The policy envisioned a region of borders blurred by increased trade and a common culture and history.

The expansionary aspects of the policy of strategic depth are also based heavily on Davutoglu's understanding of Ottoman history and his belief that the empire's political strength stemmed from the embrace of *Tawhid* (oneness with, or acceptance of, Allah) and *Tanzih* (a belief in the purity of Allah) as 'the paradigmatic base of unity among conflicting schools, sects, and traditions in Islamic history'.[13] In other words, the source of the Ottoman Empire's strength lay in the legitimacy of its ruler, itself rooted in the embrace of Islam. This provided the framework for societal harmony in the multi-ethnic and multi-religious empire. Applied to the predominantly Muslim Middle East of the twenty-first century, the concepts of *Tawhid* and *Tanzih* would therefore allow sectarian differences to be overcome, due to the fact that both are ultimately embraced by all of Islam's different sects.

Thus Davutoglu blends classic geopolitical theories with an emphasis on the role of Islam as a source of political legitimacy for many of the world's Muslim-majority countries. As such, he has argued for a return to a concept of more religiously conservative governments, reflective of the Muslim masses and congruent with the region's history. This worldview, he has argued, is at odds with the arguments made in Samuel Huntington's *The Clash of Civilizations and the Remaking of the World Order* (1996) and Francis Fukuyama's *The End of History and the Last Man* (1992), which – in his view – have been used by Western

---

[12] Ozkhan, 'Turkey, Davutoglu and the Idea of Pan-Islam', p. 123.
[13] Ahmet Davutoglu, 'The Impacts of Alternative Weltanschauungs on Political Theories: A Comparison of the Tawhid and Ontological Proximity', PhD thesis, 1990, pp. 65–67.

governments to expand their spheres of influence in the Middle East, Balkans and Caucasus.[14]

Indeed, Davutoglu contends that Western political theory is ill-suited to the Muslim world because it arrogantly assumes that individual knowledge can compete with that of Allah. He also blames the region's instability on the import of Western political constructs like ethnic nationalism,[15] arguing that the rulers who have embraced these concepts have lost their political legitimacy, having to rely instead on repression to remain in power. This repression, he asserts, is supported by the West, which fears that any change to the political status quo would undermine its own influence in the Middle East. Davutoglu sees this arrangement as ultimately unsustainable and believes that the era of political nationalism will eventually end,[16] with those governments that adopted Western constructs replaced by more representative governments that embrace *Tawhid* as the source of their political legitimacy. In other words, he argues that a conception of pan-Islamism – which he defines as being linked to a shared history and culture, which are in turn rooted in *Tawhid* and *Tanzih* – is useful for resisting what he calls the spread of Western civilisation.

To this end, Davutoglu maintains, Turkey has a unique role to play. Turkey, he argues, is not an 'ordinary state', but rather the 'centre of an [Ottoman] civilisation, which had established an original and long-lasting political order'.[17] This argument builds on Davutoglu's particular under-standing of geopolitics – and his consequent vision for the Middle East in which nationalism is replaced with a more conservative style of govern-ment premised on the legitimacy of *Tawhid*. Should this vision be realised, Middle Eastern governments would be politically and culturally linked to Turkey, thereby lessening the significance of national borders. Their embrace of *Tawhid* would also allow for the resolution of many of the region's problems, including ethnic nationalism and sectarianism. In this

---

[14] Ahmet Davutoglu, 'The Clash of Interests: An Explanation of the World [Dis]Order', *Intellectual Discourse* (Vol. 2, No. 2, 1994), pp. 107–30.

[15] Davutoglu, 'The Impacts of Alternative Weltanschauungs on Political Theories', pp. 65–67.

[16] Ahmet Davutoglu, 'Yeni dunya duzeninde Misak-i Milli', *Aksiyon*, 30 March 1996, <http://www.aksiyon.com.tr/aksiyon/columnistDetail_getNewsById.action?newsId=1431>, accessed 8 October 2014.

[17] Ahmet Davutoglu, *Stratejik Derinlik* (Istanbul: Kure Yayinlari, 2001), p. 66, as cited in Ozkhan, 'Turkey, Davutoglu and the Idea of Pan- Islamism', p. 123; Ahmet Davutoglu, 'Disisleri Bakani Sayin Ahmet Davutoglu'nun Diyarbakir Dicle Universitesinde Verdigi "Buyuk Restorasyon: Kadim'den Kuresellesmeye Yeni Siyaset Anlayisimiz"', Konulu Konferans, 15 March 2013, <http://www.mfa.gov.tr/disisleri-bakani-ahmet-davutoglu_nun-diyarbakir-dicle-universitesinde-verdigi-_buyuk-restorasyon_-kadim_den-kuresellesmeye-yeni.tr.mfa>, accessed 8 October 2014.

context, Ankara would assume its historical and natural role as a regional 'centre state', allowing it to become a global power.

This philosophy has important ramifications for Turkey's handling of the Kurdish issue, as well as for the AKP's understanding of political Islam, its foreign policy and the thinking behind its actions in the Arab Middle East.

From Philosophy to Foreign Policy: The AKP Embraces Strategic Depth

Following the AKP's election in 2002, it initially adopted a multipronged approach to foreign policy that blended certain elements of strategic depth with *realpolitik* (which the AKP dubbed *ostpolitik*, in reference to the West German Cold War-era foreign policy of normalising relations with its communist neighbour, the German Democratic Republic). The result was that Ankara's early handling of regional affairs was at times at odds with a number of Davutoglu's assertions about failed political ideologies in much of the Middle East. In Syria, Iran and the Gulf Arab states, for example, Turkey embraced the political status quo, choosing to ignore these countries' political and democratic shortcomings in favour of an emphasis on bolstering dialogue and trade. Thus, in its early foreign policy Ankara disregarded Davutoglu's belief that the era of political and ethnic nationalism was destined to fail.

However, the AKP did apply much of Davutoglu's philosophy to states that were already undergoing political transitions. In post-2003 Iraq, for example, the AKP initially sought to strengthen ties with the Iraqi Islamic Party (IIP), the political party that evolved from the Iraqi Muslim Brotherhood. In Gaza, the AKP eagerly embraced the 2006 election of Hamas, which it sought to portray as an altruistic attempt to encourage the militant group to soften its stance on Israel – although Davutoglu's own writings suggest that the group's elevation of Islam over nationalism (in contrast to the other Palestinian group, Fatah) influenced Turkey's perspective in this instance. Moreover, the group's religiosity was seen as an opportunity to deepen Turkish influence in Palestinian politics.

Beyond these two examples, Ankara's efforts to play a larger role in regional affairs from 2002 centred on its capacity to act as a neutral mediator in the region's longstanding conflicts. Thus Turkey adopted a policy of non-intervention in politically stable states in the region, alongside an interventionist approach to states undergoing political change, foreshadowing the country's policy changes after the start of the Arab upheavals, when the AKP began to implement elements of Davutoglu's foreign-policy philosophy.

Since the end of 2010, Turkey has overcome its initial reluctance to support political change in the Middle East and has adopted a pro-revolution policy with regard to Tunisia, Egypt and Syria. Moreover, in keeping with the pattern first established by the AKP in Iraq in 2005 and in Palestine in 2006, Ankara has supported the political aspirations of religiously conservative parties linked to the Muslim Brotherhood. Meanwhile, many Western countries have begun to look to Turkey to act as a 'midwife' – and a democratic political model – to the region's new, religiously conservative leaderships. As such, Ankara has faced very few constraints in formulating and implementing policy shortly before, during and after the Arab upheavals, and has actually been encouraged in its foreign-policy approach by the West.

The AKP eagerly embraced these circumstances, although going to great lengths in its rhetoric to downplay the idea of a Turkish political 'model', suggesting instead that the AKP could serve as 'inspiration' to the slew of Muslim Brotherhood-backed parties. Thus, for much of late 2012 and early 2013, the arguments Davutoglu had put forward in his numerous writings on the geopolitics of the Middle East appeared to be on the verge of coming to fruition. The optimism of the moment implied, as Davutoglu had argued, the end of nationalism as a source of Arab political legitimacy alongside the political empowerment of religiously conservative parties that espoused the development of political systems more strongly rooted in *Tawhid*. This key political shift, it was believed, would ultimately benefit Turkey, bolstering its efforts to carve out an area of influence in the Middle East and establish itself as a global power.

This optimism would not last. The start of the Syrian civil war, as well as the July 2013 coup in Egypt, precipitated a serious decline in Turkish influence in the region. Yet, despite a series of foreign-policy defeats, the AKP has shown little indication that it is willing to scale back its ambitions. The party now argues that it is playing the long game in the region and that its recent political setbacks are only temporary.

In line with this, the AKP has ascribed its foreign-policy problems to Turkey's 'precious loneliness' in the region, a phrase intended to illustrate the fact that the country is standing on the 'right side of history' in its continued support for regional democracy. Through this diagnosis, the party is drawing a clear distinction between itself and the West, which many of its members have criticised for its hands-off approach to the situation in Gaza, the Syrian civil war and the 2013 coup in Egypt. This criticism also reflects another philosophical tenet of the policy of strategic depth, namely that the West's Middle East policy is rooted in its own interest in maintaining the current political order. By contrast, the AKP casts its own actions as 'interest-free', based instead purely on the values it promotes.

II. CONSERVATIVE POLITICS AND PROBLEM-SOLVING, 2002–11

This chapter details Turkey's policies towards Syria, the Israel-Palestine question, and Iraq between 2002 and 2011, as well as the Justice and Development Party's (AKP) relationship with Iran since 2002. During this period, the AKP's foreign policy towards the Middle East incorporated aspects of the policy of 'strategic depth', while blending this with elements of Turkey's traditional policies of non-interference. This resulted in the formulation of a nuanced and country-specific policy for regional states.

Until late 2010, the AKP's regional policy followed a distinct pattern. In politically stable countries with strong central governments, such as Syria and Iran, it focused on strengthening economic and political ties. These efforts were largely successful and were heralded as major foreign-policy accomplishments prior to the Arab upheavals. In contrast, with regard to those countries undergoing political turmoil, such as Palestine and Iraq, the AKP sought to shape internal politics by supporting religiously conservative political parties linked to the Muslim Brotherhood. This approach to states in transition foreshadowed the party's handling of the region's politics during and after the Arab upheavals (as will be discussed in detail in Chapter III).

Turkey's Historical Troubles with Syria

Up until September 2011, Syria was the centrepiece of the AKP's foreign policy in the Middle East. Yet, historically, Ankara's relationship with Damascus has been problematic. During the Cold War, Syria's alliance with the Soviet Union prevented the deepening of political and economic ties. The rise of the Kurdistan Workers' Party (PKK) in Turkey from 1984 further strained relations, Syrian President Hafez Al-Assad having granted safe haven to the PKK and hosted its leader, Abdullah Ocalan, until 1998. In response, Ankara blamed Damascus for prolonging its conflict with the PKK and for contributing to the deaths of thousands of Turkish soldiers and civilians.

The dynamics of the Turkish–Syrian relationship changed in 1998. After an uptick in PKK attacks, Ankara had threatened to invade Syria to destroy the group's camps in the northeast of the country; but tension between the two subsided in October 1998 after Assad ended his support for Ocalan, thus forcing the PKK leader to flee Syria. This resulted in the two countries signing the Adana Accord, which was the first step towards political rapprochement.

The signing of the agreement enabled Turkish businessmen and policy-makers to seek to bolster ties with their counterparts in Damascus. In 2000, Turkey's then-President Ahmet Necdet Sezer visited Damascus for the funeral of Hafez Al-Assad, signalling to incoming Syrian President Bashar Al-Assad that Turkey was committed to furthering the political rapprochement. Between 2000 and 2003, Turkish officials met with their Syrian counterparts some thirty times to help deepen political and economic ties.

The AKP's Syria Policy: Embracing *Ostpolitik*

With the election of the AKP in 2002, Turkey's rapprochement with Syria became more firmly entrenched. Ankara prioritised the strengthening of ties with Assad, despite its own rejection of the Ba'athist ideology, which views secular Arab nationalism, rather than Islam, as the source of political legitimacy.

This accommodation of the Ba'athists, at least initially, can be explained in part by recourse to Davutolgu's philosophy. Although, in his view, the creation of new states in the Middle East after the First World War helped to empower a secular ruling class whose worldview was incongruent with that of the people it governed, it would take time to phase out the political ideology of parties such as the Ba'athists, which was well entrenched. Indeed, Davutoglu has argued that the Cold War's bipolar order was one of the reasons for the widespread appeal of Ba'athism in Syria. The East–West divide, he postulated, allowed external powers to use proxies to create conflict in the Middle East. In Syria, Davutoglu suggested, the disagreement over Turkey's water policies in the southeast, as well as Damascus's support for the PKK were, in part, explained by the protection afforded to Syria by the Soviet Union. In turn, Hafez Al-Assad had used this tension to increase his nationalist appeal, thereby increasing his own political legitimacy. Thus although he thought that, following the end of the Cold War, Ba'athism would be replaced by a different political ideology (given that the reasons for Turkish–Syrian friction had been removed), he also believed that this change would take place over time. In the interim, therefore, Turkey's best course of action would be to pursue closer economic ties with Syria, regardless of ideology.[1]

The AKP was also acutely aware of the limits to Turkish power, given that the country did not have the military strength, political means or economic might to seriously upset the regional status quo. Turkey therefore settled on a Syria policy that Davutoglu described as akin to West Germany's *ostpolitik*, in reference to its Cold War détente with Soviet-controlled East Germany.[2] This resulted in Turkey prioritising its economic and political interests in Syria rather than focusing on pressuring Assad to make political changes.[3] However, it also implied an underlying ideological antagonism and a sense that one day the regime would fall.

By using *ostpolitik* as its guide, Davutoglu expected Turkey to regain its influence in Syria, not least because he also credited *ostpolitik* with helping to end the Soviet Union's control over Eastern Europe.[4] In his 2001 book *Stratejic Derinlik* (hereafter *Strategic Depth*), Davutoglu wrote that improved Turkish–Syrian economic ties would allow Turkish businesses based in Anatolia to expand into Syria, and would thus reconnect the Syrian city of Aleppo with its natural hinterland in southern Anatolia.[5] In turn, the Turkish cities of Kahramanmaras, Gaziantep and Urfa would benefit from increased trade and the easing of visa restrictions, whilst Turkey would gain greater influence over the Syrian government. Finally, a more co-operative relationship with Syria would enable Turkish exporters to ship products over land via Syrian territory to the lucrative markets of the Arab Gulf states.

Thus, after coming to power in 2002, the AKP immediately prioritised the relationship with Syria, eager to convince Turkey's erstwhile adversary to deepen economic and cultural ties, and to move beyond the antagonisms that had dominated the relationship until 1998. This policy had its roots in previous efforts after the signing of the Adana Accord, but the AKP's embrace of Bashar Al-Assad was the centrepiece of its new foreign-policy agenda.

In January 2004, Assad travelled to Turkey on an official state visit – the first by a Syrian president in fifty-seven years. During the visit, the two

---

[1] Ahmet Davutoglu, *Stratejic Derinlik* (Istanbul: Kure Yayinlari, 2001), pp. 362–63.
[2] Ahmet Davutoglu, 'Ortadogu meselesinde yeni projeksiyonlar ve Türkiye', *Yeni Safak*, 24 February 1999, <http://yenisafak.com.tr:999/yazarlar/AhmetDavutoglu/ortadogu-meselesinde-yeni-projeksiyonlar-ve-turkiye/40598>, accessed 10 October 2014.
[3] Owen Matthews, 'Davutoglu: Inside Turkey's New Foreign Policy', *Newsweek*, 28 November 2009.
[4] Mehmet Yilmaz, 'Derin Bir Kitap', *Zaman*, 4 June 2001.
[5] Davutoglu, *Stratejik Derinlik*, p. 372.

sides signed a number of agreements, including the Agreement on Avoidance of Double Taxation and the Agreement on Reciprocal Promotion and Protection of Investment.

The two countries also shared an interest in preventing the establishment of an independent Kurdish state in Iraq. Indeed, following the US-led invasion of Iraq in 2003, this prospect was a worrying one for both Syria and Turkey. Both have large Kurdish populations and were thus eager to stifle any semblance of Kurdish political empowerment. During Assad's visit to Turkey in 2004, he told *CNN Turk*, 'if there is no territorial integrity in Iraq, we cannot talk about stability in Iraq or in our countries … We are not only against a Kurdish state, but any state that would break the integrity of Iraq.'[6] Turkish President Sezer publicly echoed these sentiments.[7] Syria's embrace of Iraqi territorial integrity was certainly self-interested. However, having supported the PKK until 1998, the Syrian government's adoption of a policy similar to Ankara's certainly helped to assuage lingering suspicions of the Turkish security establishment. This provided enough breathing space for the AKP to pursue a more comprehensive foreign policy aimed at deepening ties with Damascus.

In December 2004, Turkey's then-Prime Minister Recep Tayyip Erdogan visited Damascus for another high-level meeting. Before this trip, he told reporters that a 'new era had begun' in relations with Syria and that 'god willing, during this visit we will take political and economic steps that will add to our bilateral ties'.[8] During the visit, Turkey and Syria signed a free-trade agreement that eventually came into force in 2007.[9] Later, in 2006, the two sides also agreed to eliminate visa requirements.[10] This easing of visa and trade restrictions led to a rapid increase in Turkish–Syrian trade. In 2002, bilateral trade stood at $773 million. By 2010, it had grown to over $2.27 billion. Erdogan heralded the new era in December 2004 by asking of his Syrian audience: 'Is it possible to differentiate a Syrian and a Turk among the people of enlightened faces in this hall? I want to call you not my friends but my brothers.'[11]

---

[6] Louis Meixler, 'Syrian, Turkish Leaders Meet amid Concern over Kurds in Iraq', *Associated Press*, 6 January 2004.

[7] *Ibid.*

[8] *Agence France Presse*, 'Turkish PM Visits Former Foe Syria in "New Era" of Warming Ties', 22 December 2004.

[9] Republic of Turkey: Ministry of Economy, 'Turkey–Syria Association Agreement', 22 December 2004, <http://www.economy.gov.tr/index.cfm?sayfa=tradeagreements&bolum=fta&country=SY&region=0>, accessed 10 October 2014.

[10] Meliha Benli Altunisik and Ozlem Tür, 'From Distant Neighbors to Partners? Changing Syrian-Turkish Relations', *Security Dialogue* (Vol. 37, No. 2, June 2006), p. 245.

[11] *Ibid.*

The AKP argued that its increased bilateral engagement with Syria also bolstered Turkish influence in Damascus and Aleppo – the latter Syria's largest city and the focus of much of Turkey's investment in Syria.[12]

It was this perspective that prompted the AKP to step forward as a regional mediator. Davutoglu postulated that after the collapse of the Soviet Union, the two major geopolitical issues facing the Middle East were the Israel–Palestine conflict and the competition for resources. Turkey, he argued, must help to shape the outcome in these two areas – and thus ensure that the solution comes from within the region; the alternative would risk having outside powers dictate the course of regional events. This diplomatic activity, in turn, would once again place Turkey at the centre of regional policy-making, rehabilitating it from its position as a peripheral power in its historical hinterland.

In line with this, the AKP sought increasingly to mediate Israel's conflicts with both Syria and the Palestinians. In 2004, at the request of the Syrian government, the AKP announced its willingness to mediate peace discussions between Jerusalem and Damascus. Shortly thereafter, Israel publicly acknowledged its acceptance of Turkish mediation.[13]

The first indirect peace talks were held in Istanbul in May 2008.[14] The two parties met another four times between May and July 2008, before negotiations were temporarily suspended in July, after Israel's then-Prime Minister Ehud Olmert was questioned about illegal campaign contributions.[15] In December 2008, Olmert visited Ankara, where he met with Erdogan at his personal residence. During this meeting, Erdogan is reported to have been on the phone with Assad, working to help bridge the gaps between the two parties.

This meeting coincided with a surge in violence in the Gaza Strip, which eventually resulted in Israel launching a ground invasion of Gaza, dubbed Operation *Cast Lead*. The Turkish prime minister had reportedly asked Olmert not to escalate the conflict and personally passed on an urgent request by Hamas leader Ismail Haniyeh to lift the Israeli blockade of Gaza and halt military operations.[16] Olmert refused, citing the ongoing rocket fire. Given Erdogan's personal efforts – primarily to push the Syrians and the

---

[12] Khaled Yacoub Oweis, 'Trade Flourishes as Syria Befriends Old Foe Turkey', *Reuters*, 4 June 2010.

[13] Hazel Ward, 'Israel Prepares for Prisoner Swap as Turkey Offers to Mediate with Syria', *Agence France Presse*, 25 January 2004.

[14] *Agence France Presse*, 'Israel, Syria "Satisfied" with Talks: Turkish FM', 22 May 2008.

[15] Rory McCarthy, 'Olmert Questioned Again as Police Widen Corruption Inquiry', *Guardian*, 12 July 2008.

[16] 'Turkey/Israel/Syria: Olmert Remains Positive on Turkish Mediated Talks, but Time Running Out', diplomatic cable, 24 December 2008, <https://www.wikileaks.org/plusd/cables/08ANKARA2174_a.html>, accessed 21 October 2014.

Israelis to continue to negotiate in order to demonstrate that the Turkish-facilitated 'indirect talks [had] produced a concrete result'[17] – Israel's launch of a ground incursion left Erdogan feeling personally betrayed. He was also acutely aware that his recent meeting with Olmert could give the impression of Turkish complicity in the Israeli assault. Erdogan consequently expressed his outrage at the Israeli escalation, saying, 'Today, I was planning to call Israeli Prime Minister Olmert regarding Israel–Syria talks but I cancelled it. I am not calling because it is also disrespectful to us. We are a country which has been working for peace.'[18]

The surge in Israeli–Palestinian violence also ended Turkish-led efforts to broker an agreement between Jerusalem and Damascus. On 28 December 2008, Syria suspended its participation in the peace talks. An unnamed Syrian official responded to Erdogan's comments about Israeli military action, noting that, 'After what the Turkish side said, Israel's aggression against Gaza closes all the doors in front of any move toward a settlement in the region'.[19] The next day, Turkey announced that it was ending its efforts to advance the still-nascent peace discussions. As stated by Ali Babacan, Turkey's foreign minister from August 2007 to May 2009, 'the continuation of the talks under these conditions is naturally impossible'.[20] The talks were never resuscitated, despite the (admittedly limited) progress made by the parties, suggesting that they were incredibly fragile from the outset.

Ankara Embraces Hamas

Turkey has historically been sympathetic to Palestinian political empowerment,[21] despite the fact that for much of the Cold War it largely disengaged from the issue, focusing instead on its relationship with the West. Since 2002, however, the AKP has pursued a different policy, viewing Palestine as 'an area of responsibility' within Turkish foreign policy.[22] In *Strategic Depth*, Davutoglu praises Hamas and credits the group with advancing the cause of Palestinian statehood in the years immediately after the First Intifada (1987–93). Yet, despite these ingrained

---

[17] *Ibid.*

[18] Paul Schemm, 'Arab World Condemns Israeli Attack on Gaza', *Associated Press*, 27 December 2008.

[19] Albert Aji, 'Syria Suspends Indirect Peace Talks with Israel', *Associated Press*, 28 December 2008.

[20] *Agence France Presse*, 'Turkey Ends Israel–Syria Peace Effort Over Gaza Offensive', 29 December 2008.

[21] Meliha Altunisik, 'The Turkish–Israeli Rapprochement in the Post-Cold War Era', *Middle Eastern Studies* (Vol. 36, No. 2, April 2000), pp. 172–91.

[22] Bulent Aras and Rabia Karakaya Polat, 'Turkey and the Middle East: Frontiers of the New Geographic Imagination', *Australian Journal of International Affairs* (Vol. 61, No. 4, 2007), p. 478.

sympathies for Hamas, Turkey's initial Israel-Palestine policy required close co-operation with Israel and Fatah, the Palestinian political movement in control of the West Bank led by Mahmoud Abbas. Following numerous bouts of Israeli–Palestinian violence and the 2006 election in Palestine, however, the AKP adopted a pro-Hamas policy, based primarily on the argument that the group was more representative of the Palestinian people and politically more successful than Fatah. The evolution of the AKP's Palestine policy foreshadowed its handling of regional events after the Arab upheavals and was an early indication of both Ankara's position on political Islam and its troubles with the West's approach to parties linked to the Muslim Brotherhood.

Meanwhile, Turkey's bilateral interactions with Israel have proven troublesome on occasion in the last two decades. After the end of the Cold War, Turkey's desire for advanced weapons, combined with a brief moment of optimism regarding the Israeli-Palestinian peace process, helped to facilitate the conclusion of three separate Turkish–Israeli military co-operation agreements in 1996. The first of these agreements was signed in February of that year, shortly after Erbakan's election and formal advocacy for his Developing-8 (D-8) project, which was conceived as an Islamic counterpoint to what was then the G7 and included Turkey, Egypt, Bangladesh, Indonesia, Iran, Malaysia, Nigeria and Pakistan as members.

The first agreement was initially kept secret, but was leaked to the Israeli press in early April, reportedly by an Israeli general eager to embarrass the Islamist Erbakan.[23] In reaction, Davutoglu, in a column for the conservative Turkish daily *Yeni Safak*, argued that the agreement was disadvantageous for Turkish security because it undermined Ankara's relationship with Iran, Syria and Iraq, and helped to enhance Ankara's dependence on the 'US-Israel' axis for its security.[24] Taha Ozhan, an adviser to Davutoglu, has subsequently described this axis as the 'Camp David Order', which he defines as the West's unwavering support for the Arab leaders who have dominated Middle Eastern affairs for the last three decades. According to Ozhan, 'This status quo positioned Israel at the centre of regional relations, and in subsequent years has enabled regional dictators to rule with an iron fist'.[25] The Israel–Palestine conflict, it was therefore argued, helps to sustain the region's autocratic status quo and continues to keep regional countries like Turkey on the periphery of regional decision-making.

---

[23] Philip Robins, *Suits and Uniforms: Turkish Foreign Policy since the End of the Cold War* (Seattle, WA: University of Washington Press, 2003), pp. 257–69.

[24] Ahmet Davutoglu, 'Turkiye Israil Guvenlik Anlasmasi ve Yeni Dengeler', *Yeni Safak*, 9 April 1996.

[25] Taha Ozhan, 'The Arab Spring and Turkey: The Camp David Order vs. the New Middle East', *Insight Turkey* (Vol. 13, No. 4, Summer 2011), pp. 55–64.

The resolution of the Israel-Palestine issue was thus seen as a way of reversing this dynamic. Furthermore, it would obviously be preferable if the conditions necessary for the resolution of this issue were to be generated from within the region itself, rather than being imposed by external actors who did not share Ankara's point of view on regional affairs. These efforts required the AKP – at least between 2002 and 2010 – to maintain cordial ties with Israel.

In this way, the concept of *ostpolitik* underpinned the AKP's relationship with Israel until 2010. However, in the Palestinian territories, the AKP clearly supported Hamas over its rival, Fatah – viewing Hamas as a legitimate political organisation working to advance the cause of an independent Palestine. Turkey's policy was ultimately aided by Western intervention in Palestine: in 2005, the US in particular pushed the Palestinian Authority, led by Fatah, to organise parliamentary elections, which were held in the following January. The resulting electoral victory by Hamas – which gained a clear majority – came as a surprise to the US, prompting it to threaten to withhold aid to the Palestinian Authority unless Hamas renounced its anti-Israel positions.[26] By contrast, Erdogan argued that 'Hamas should be given a chance' and warned that its embrace of electoral politics 'should not be blocked by prejudice', else the group might turn to 'a different process' to advance its political goals.[27] This difference in opinion is indicative of a far wider schism between the US and the EU on the one hand and Turkey on the other with regard to the role of political Islam in the Middle East, with Turkey also interpreting the West's refusal to support the group as an indication of its intent to pursue the empowerment of its preferred political actors.[28]

During an interview many years later, in March 2012, Davutoglu explicitly drew out what he saw as the tensions between the two approaches, commenting that Turkey was 'now beyond out-dated prejudices and concerns against political parties with Islamic references'.[29] The AKP, Davutoglu noted, believes that the 'democratically elected political entities should be allowed to assume and execute their govern-mental functions'. The West's refusal to allow Hamas to govern in 2006,

---

[26] Steven R Weisman, 'US Digs in on Withholding Aid to Hamas Government', *New York Times*, 17 February 2006.
[27] *Agence France Presse*, 'Turkish PM Says Hamas Should be Given a Chance', 27 January 2006.
[28] Taha Ozhan, for example, argued in 2014 that the steps taken after the 2006 election were a 'military coup co-sponsored by the West and Israel'. See Taha Ozhan, 'The Limited Victory of Tunisian Islamists', *Daily Sabah*, 7 November 2014.
[29] Republic of Turkey, Ministry of Foreign Affairs, 'Interview by Mr. Ahmet Davutolu published in AUC Cairo Review (Egypt) on 12 March 2012', <http://www.mfa.gov.tr/interview-by-mr_-ahmet-davutoglu-published-in-auc-cairo-review-_egypt_-on-12-march-2012.en.mfa>, accessed 30 October 2014.

Davutoglu argued in the same interview, was in part responsible for the violence between Fatah and Hamas that followed, negatively affecting the peace process.[30]

A month after the 2006 Palestinian elections, in February, Turkey invited Hamas leader Khaled Meshaal and four of his associates to Ankara for meetings with senior AKP officials (although the Hamas leader was prevented from meeting with Erdogan after word of his visit was leaked to the Turkish press).[31] At the time, Hamas and Fatah had yet to form a government and low-level clashes between the two parties' militias had already begun. These clashes eventually resulted in the de facto separation of Palestine between Hamas-run Gaza and the Fatah-run West Bank. In response to criticism by the US for meeting with Meshaal, Turkey framed its support for Hamas as a simple reflection of its broader support for the democratic process in the region, and its efforts to moderate the group's position. Indeed, then-Foreign Minister Abdullah Gul encouraged Hamas to renounce violence, reiterated Ankara's long-standing support for a two-state solution, and encouraged the group to come to the table in order to negotiate a peaceful resolution to the Israeli–Palestinian conflict.[32]

The AKP's persistent support for Hamas can largely be explained by its views on, and preference for, political Islam. In *Strategic Depth*, written in 2001, Davutoglu implied that the First Intifada had been akin to the mass rebellions in Eastern Europe towards the end of the Cold War and part of a much broader struggle within the Muslim world for greater democratic and religious freedoms. These demands, Davutoglu had previously argued in 1994, 'resulted in the increase of the role of Islamic values and institutions in the political system' and have 'synchronized the demands for the processes of democratization and Islamization'. In the Muslim world, these efforts exacerbated the tensions between 'secular political/bureaucratic elites' and 'Islamic Socio-Political forces'.[33]

This narrative helps to explain why the AKP does not view Hamas, which was founded by Sheikh Ahmed Yassin during the First Intifada, as a terrorist organisation, instead seeing it a legitimate political party whose political views are widely shared by its constituency. The group's history of violence was framed within the context of Israel's actions in Palestine and was therefore excused. It also explains why the AKP eagerly sought to

---

[30] Republic of Turkey, Ministry of Foreign Affairs, 'Interview by Mr. Ahmet Davutoglu Published in AUC Cairo Review (Egypt) on 12 March 2012'.

[31] *Los Angeles Times*, 'Turkey Allows Hamas Visit', 17 February 2006.

[32] Selcan Hacaoglu, 'Hamas Political Leader Mashaal Meets with Turkish Officials', *Associated Press*, 16 February 2006.

[33] Ahmet Davutoglu, 'Rewriting Contemporary Muslim Politics: A Twentieth Century Periodization', in Fred Dallmayr (ed.), *Border Crossings: Toward a Comparative Political Theory* (New York, NY: Lexington Books, 1999), p. 105.

support Hamas after its election victory in 2006, even though doing so overtly risked damaging its ties with both Israel and Fatah. Moreover, in *Strategic Depth*, Davutoglu had described Fatah as one of the many political parties that relied on 'secular nationalism' in its attempts to build a new national identity after the founding of the Palestine Liberation Organization (PLO) in 1964. This nationalism, Davutoglu argued as early as 2001, would fail in Palestine if there was a fair, democratic process in the Arab world.[34] The AKP, therefore, has interpreted the Israel–Palestine conflict within its overarching belief in the imminent decline of nationalism as a source of political legitimacy and the inevitable replacement of the old elites with a new crop of conservative leaders.

In line with this, the AKP had few reasons to maintain close relations with the Jewish state, which Davutoglu had argued in 1996 would undermine Turkey's position with its Muslim-majority neighbours.[35] Furthermore, some areas within these neighbouring territories, in Iraq and Syria for instance, are thought of by the AKP as Turkey's natural hinterland, and are therefore viewed as critical for the implementation of the policy of strategic depth. Thus, during times of crisis, the AKP's leadership has shown little restraint when criticising Israel. In late January 2009, for example, Erdogan publicly chastised Israel's then-President Shimon Peres, whilst the two were speaking on a panel at the World Economic Forum in Davos,[36] for his passionate defence of Israel's recent Operation *Cast Lead* in Gaza, saying, 'When it comes to killing, you know well how to kill'.[37]

Erdogan's rhetoric and Israel's actions in Gaza subsequently continued to undermine relations with Israel's leadership. In the aftermath of Operation *Cast Lead*, which resulted in 1,400 Palestinians being killed,[38] Turkey cancelled a planned joint military exercise with Israel.[39] In 2010, the religiously conservative Turkish charity Insan Hak ve Hurriyetleri ve Insani Yardim Vakfi (IHH) – which has no formal links to the AKP, but whose board includes AKP members of parliament and people affiliated with the party[40] – organised a large flotilla of ships to deliver aid to the Gaza Strip.

---

[34] Davutoglu, *Stratejik Derinlik*, pp. 366–67.

[35] Davutoglu, 'Turkiye Israil Guvenlik Anlasmasi ve Yeni Dengeler'.

[36] *Guardian*, 'Recep Erdogan Storms out of Davos after Clash with Israeli President over Gaza', 30 January 2009.

[37] Kathrin Benhold, 'Leaders of Turkey and Israel Clash at Davos Panel', *New York Times*, 29 January 2009.

[38] Amnesty International, 'Operation Cast Lead: 22 Days of Death and Destruction', 2 July 2009.

[39] Julian Borger, 'Turkey Confirms it Barred Israel from Military Exercise because of Gaza War', *Guardian*, 12 October 2009.

[40] Melis Tusiray and Michael Werz, 'What is the IHH?', Center for American Progress, 26 July 2010.

The Israeli government maintained a strict blockade of the area and ultimately decided to use military force to prevent the ships from entering the port of Gaza. During the operation, Israeli soldiers killed nine Turkish citizens onboard the *Mavi Marmara*, the flotilla's largest ship. In the wake of the tragedy, Ankara severed diplomatic relations with Israel and suspended all military agreements.[41] As many as ten AKP members of parliament had considered joining the flotilla before it departed for Gaza, but were barred from doing so by the Turkish Foreign Ministry at the last minute. However, the IHH organisers were greeted at the airport upon their return by Bulent Arinc, then-deputy prime minister and one of the original founders of the AKP.[42]

Turkey subsequently placed numerous conditions on the resumption of diplomatic ties, demanding that Israel apologise, pay compensation to the victims' families, and end its blockade of Gaza.[43] This final demand had also been made by Hamas during Erdogan's 2008 meeting with Olmert. At that time, Turkey was willing to overlook this demand, and instead focused on advancing its efforts to facilitate indirect Syrian–Israeli peace negotiations. The *Mavi Marmara* incident thus saw the alignment of Ankara's and Hamas's demands in relation to Israel's blockade of Gaza.

By adopting such overtly pro-Hamas policies, Turkey has undermined its ability to act as a neutral mediator in relation to the Israel–Palestine conflict. However, these same policies have engendered tremendous sympathy from many people in the Arab world. Thus, while Ankara's support for Hamas has placed it at odds with many of its Western allies, its support for the militant group has increased the appeal of the AKP in many Muslim-majority countries.

This schism speaks to a broader point: as Ankara's popularity surged in the years before the start of the Syrian conflict in 2011, Turkey felt that this would lead to an increase in its influence within the Middle East. However, this was not to be. On the contrary, as will be discussed in Chapter III, Turkey's policy of support for Hamas eventually resulted in its losing leverage with much of the region's leadership. However, its policy position seems unlikely to change, given that the AKP continues to argue that its support for Hamas and the Palestinian cause will pay off in the future. Instead, Turkey is likely to continue to put pressure on Israel to

---

[41] Republic of Turkey, Ministry of Foreign Affairs, 'Relations between Turkey and Israel, Ministry of Foreign Affairs', <http://www.mfa.gov.tr/relations-between-turkey-and-israel%20.en.mfa>, accessed 7 November 2014.

[42] Dan Bilefsky and Sebnem Arsu, 'Sponsor of Flotilla Tied to Elite of Turkey', *New York Times*, 15 July 2010.

[43] Yigal Schleifer, 'Turkey: Relations with Israel Hit Rock Bottom', *Eurasianet*, 2 September 2011.

make concessions that would facilitate Hamas's efforts to create an independent Palestine.

The Decline of Ankara's Influence in Baghdad

The 2003 invasion of Iraq by the US and UK posed a unique challenge for the recently elected AKP government. The US had initially envisioned amassing troops and equipment in southern Turkey to invade Iraq along a second front (the first being through Kuwait). After then-Prime Minister Gul had travelled through the region to rally Arab support for a plan to force Saddam Hussein to comply with the demands of the UN Security Council, Erdogan and Gul initially decided to support the US plan to station tens of thousands of its troops on Turkish territory. They were following the advice of the Turkish military, which although opposed to the invasion, felt that it made sense for Turkey to support the operation, given the US's determination over the matter.[44] The AKP-led cabinet appeared to signal its support for the invasion and, in anticipation of a positive vote in parliament, agreed to allow the US to offload some equipment in the port of Iskenderun in preparation for the deployment of some 9,000 vehicles and 40,000 US troops on Turkish soil.[45]

However, Bulent Arinc, then-speaker of the parliament, was deeply opposed to the war and refused to rally support for the invasion. At the time, Erdogan had not yet become prime minister, owing to legal issues surrounding a previous arrest in 1998.[46] Absent a strong leader, the party revolted against Erdogan's preferred policy, with 100 members rebelling and the assembly ultimately rejecting the motion that would have allowed the US to use Turkish territory to launch an invasion.[47] In spite of this result, in a positive signal to the US, Erdogan, shortly after taking office, convinced parliament to allow the US both overflight rights from airbases in Turkey and overland resupply routes for the occupation forces.[48]

Turkey sought to play a more pronounced role in Iraqi politics after the drafting of the Iraqi constitution and the scheduling of two elections in

---

[44] William Hale, *Turkish Foreign Policy since 1774*, 3rd edition (London: Routledge, 2013), p. 166.
[45] Dexter Filkins, 'Turkey's Cabinet Approves Plan, with Details Lacking, for U.S. Troops', *New York Times*, 25 February 2003.
[46] *The Economist,* 'A Pivotal Nation Goes into a Spin', 6 March 2003.
[47] James Kapsis, 'The Failure of U.S.-Turkish Pre-Iraq War Negotiations: An Overconfident United States, Political Mismanagement, and A Conflicted Military', Gloria Center, IDC Herziliya, 3 September 2006.
[48] *Associated Press*, 'Turkey Agrees to U.S. Overflights for Iraq War', 21 March 2003.

2005. Indeed, the AKP was instrumental in helping to ensure the passage of the Iraqi constitution that year, despite its increasing concerns over the alienation of Iraqi Sunnis from the country's political process and the language used in Iraq's constitution.[49] With US support, the AKP hosted Tariq Al-Hashimi, the leader of the Iraqi Islamic Party (IIP) – the Iraqi branch of the Muslim Brotherhood – at a major conference in Istanbul to help convince the IIP and the three other Sunni groups to vote in favour of the constitution at the upcoming referendum.[50] Davutoglu has since celebrated Turkey's role in the process, writing that his mediation efforts had resulted in the parties forming the Tawafuq ('consensus') political coalition – comprising the IIP (as the dominant party), Ahl Al-Iraq and the National Dialogue Council – and had thus helped to secure political support for the constitution.[51]

Ankara supported the IIP for three reasons. First, the AKP favoured the IIP's politics, which advocated the creation of a unified and highly centralised Iraq, based on an Islamic identity.[52] Second, it was the dominant member of the only major Sunni political bloc to embrace electoral politics between 2005 and 2009. Third, Ankara hoped to bolster the party as a counterweight to the Kurds and their claims to Mosul in Iraq's Nineveh Province, as well as to provide the foundation for a more coherent Sunni opposition that could eventually challenge the Iranian-backed Shia bloc then governing in Baghdad.[53]

After the passage of the constitution, the AKP pursued a multi-pronged foreign policy focused on helping to create a political system in Iraq that would allow for Turkey to extend its influence. This meant that Turkey had to take steps to try to empower a Sunni political bloc capable of bridging the country's sectarian divide while also currying favour with the emerging Shia political parties; in 2009, for example, it hosted Shia cleric Muqtada Al-Sadr at the Cankaya Presidential Palace in Ankara.[54] This policy was, in turn, based on the assumption that Turkey and Iran are

---

[49] In 2008, for example, Davutoglu chided the US-supported constitution, stating that 'the main problem in the Iraqi constitution is that it defines different ethnicities, different sects … and it creates its own dilemma … Iraq became another Lebanon because of ethnic and sectarian definitions'. See Ahmet Davutoglu, 'Turkey's Top Foreign Policy Aide Worries about False Optimism in Iraq', Council on Foreign Relations, 19 September 2008.
[50] Burcu Ersekerci, 'Turkey Gets USA and Sunnis of Iraq Together', *Journal of Turkish Weekly*, 5 December 2005.
[51] Ahmet Davutoglu, 'Turkey's Mediation: Critical Reflections from the Field', *Middle East Policy* (Vol. 20, No. 1, Spring 2013), p. 84.
[52] *Ibid.*
[53] International Crisis Group (ICG), 'Iraq: Allaying Turkey's Fears Over Kurdish Ambitions', Middle East Report No. 35, 26 January 2005.
[54] 'Turkish Media Reaction, 4 May 2009', <https://www.wikileaks.org/plusd/cables/09ANKARA641_a.html>, accessed 21 October 2014.

ultimately in competition for influence in the Middle East (discussed in more detail later in the chapter), and on the AKP's view of Iran as a destabilising power.[55] The AKP therefore began to take steps to create an alternative political model that would weaken the Islamic Republic's influence over the country's Shia-majority political parties. To do so, Turkey sought to portray itself as a non-sectarian actor which had the interests of Iraq at the centre of its efforts, while also taking steps to organise a coherent and credible Sunni opposition.

In the years after 2005, the AKP therefore advised Iraq's Sunni population to participate in the political process and began to host a number of Sunni-majority tribes for conferences and training. Yet, despite Ankara's efforts, only the Sunni-majority Tawafuq and its supporters participated in the 2005 election. The boycott by other Sunnis allowed the Kurdistan Democratic Party (KDP) and the Patriotic Union of Kurdistan (PUK) to gain political control over Nineveh Province. The Kurdish political bloc won thirty-one out of a possible forty-one seats, compared to just two for the Turkish-supported IIP. In turn, the two Kurdish political parties began to force Arab police forces from the city, eventually pushing to limit the power of Iraqi security forces in the area more generally.[56] The result was that many disaffected Sunnis from Mosul gravitated towards the insurgency against coalition troops that was just beginning to flourish, allying with a collection of Ba'athist and Islamist militias. Turkey maintained its support for a strong central government and, in an act of symbolic defiance, the AKP opened a large consulate on the Arab-controlled west bank of Mosul in 2006.

The Sunni decision to participate in both the 2009 provincial elections and the 2010 parliamentary elections helped to advance Turkish policy in Iraq, as Ankara found common cause with Iraq's Nujaifi brothers. Neither brother was a member of the IIP, but both were aligned with the Islamic current in Iraq on most major issues.[57] Osama Al-Nujaifi was a

---

[55] Tarik Oguzlu, 'Turkey's Northern Iraq Policy: Competing Perspectives', *Insight Turkey* (Vol. 10, No. 3, 2008), p. 12.

[56] Anthony H Cordesman, Adam Mausner and Elena Derby, *Iraq and the United States: Creating a Strategic Partnership* (Washington, DC: Center for Strategic and International Studies, 2010), p. 60.

[57] ICG, 'Iraq's New Battlefront: The Struggle over Ninewa', Middle East Report No. 90, 28 September 2009. According to Kirk Sowell, the editor of *Inside Iraqi Politics*, 'Osama Nujayfi is not a formal member of the Islamic Party, but is on good terms with them and is generally referred to as being aligned with the Islamic current in Iraq. He doesn't push any kind of specific Islamist agenda, talk about Islamic law, or anything like that, though he does talk in interviews about representing "moderate Islam" as against "extremists". In a recent interview Osama Nujaifi defended the AKP in the same terms, saying they were "moderate Islam" while the Islamic State represented extremism. Also, they worked very closely with the clerics in Ninawa during the 2012 protests, and the Mutahidun are the only Sunni

member of the Iraqiya Alliance – a political coalition mostly comprised of Sunni political parties that campaigned on an overtly non-sectarian political platform, with a focus on maintaining a strong and centralised federal government.[58] His brother, Atheel Al-Nujaifi, headed the Al-Hadbaa Party, which went on to win the majority of votes in Nineveh Province during the 2009 election, and thereby secured administrative control over the province. Atheel's campaign embraced a decidedly anti-Kurdish policy in Mosul, in favour of greater political centralisation in Baghdad and the maintenance of Arab control over the city.[59]

From 2009, in anticipation of the March 2010 parliamentary elections, Turkey worked closely with Qatar, the UAE and Saudi Arabia to support the formation of Iraqiya.[60] However, this overt support for Iraqiya, both before and after the election, undermined the AKP's relationship with the Shia-dominated Dawa Party – the dominant political party in the governing State of Law coalition – and its leader, then-Prime Minister Nouri Al-Maliki.

Turkey's 2009 decision to help in the creation of Iraqiya ultimately led to the failure of its Iraq policy. Thereafter, its influence over Iraqi Shia groups declined.[61] Ankara had a tremendous amount to gain by maintaining cordial relations with Dawa in Baghdad; indeed, Iraq's demographics mean that Shia parties are certain to retain considerable political power in Iraq for the foreseeable future. Far from ensuring it retained some influence over the central government of its neighbour, however, Ankara overreached itself in opting overtly to favour a Sunni bloc.

The AKP's reasons for supporting Iraqiya at the expense of its relations with Iraq's Shia political parties are therefore worth exploring. By 2009, Ankara had grown tired of the Shia dominance of Baghdad and felt that its interests would be best served by the election of a Sunni political bloc that emphasised pan-Iraqi nationalism. Iraqiya had also proven more appealing to Iraqi Sunnis than Ankara's erstwhile ally, the IIP – with its

---

party that have [sic] any relationship with the clerics; the other Sunni factions steer clear of them entirely'. E-mail correspondence, 18 October 2014.

[58] ICG, 'Iraq's Secular Opposition: The Rise and Decline of Al-Iraqiya', Middle East Report No. 127, 31 July 2012.

[59] For example, in 2009, the AKP invited Shia cleric Muqtada Al-Sadr to Ankara for talks with then-Prime Minister Erdogan and then-Foreign Minister Davutoglu in Ankara. See *Al Jazeera*, 'Iraq's Al Sadr Visits Turkey', 2 May 2009. Similarly, in 2013, Davutoglu travelled to Najaf and Karbala in Iraq, where he met with Al-Sadr and Shia cleric Ayatollah Ali Al-Sistani. See *Today's Zaman*, 'Sectarian Clashes Must Be Prevented, Says Davutoglu', 11 November 2013.

[60] ICG, 'Iraq's Secular Opposition'.

[61] According to a former parliamentarian with the Kurdistan Islamic Union, 'Turkey, backed by the UAE and Qatar, took the lead in supporting Iraqiya, so that Iran would not feel it was an Arab initiative'. *Ibid.*

leader, Tariq Al-Hashemi, later forming the 'Renewal Party', which then ran on Iraqiya's list in 2010.

Turkey's policy was initially successful. Iraqiya won ninety-one out of 325 seats in Iraq's Council of Representatives, compared to the eighty-nine won by Maliki's State of Law coalition. In spite of this, however, Maliki was able to retain his position as prime minister because of the support he received from Iraq's other Shia parties and Iran.[62] Iraqiya members of parliament were subsequently handed a number of ministerial positions; but Maliki soon sidestepped these via the consolidation of power in the office of the prime minister.

Iraqiya eventually collapsed in 2012, after which Turkey backed Osama Al-Nujaifi's Mutahidun party. However, the party has failed to attract significant support and lost eighteen of its forty-five seats in Iraq's 2014 national election.[63] Indeed, the persistent success of Dawa has been a tremendous setback for Turkish foreign policy, with Ankara's favoured political actors having failed to seriously challenge Shia dominance in Baghdad. The result is that Turkey's influence has declined and, as in other countries, it became tied completely to the success of a few individuals whose popularity was also waning.

These twin failures prompted Ankara to focus instead on its relationship with the KDP in Iraq's Kurdistan Regional Government (KRG). It was in 2005 that the KDP, led by Masoud Barzani, had first approached Turkey about developing closer economic and energy relations. The KDP's reasons for doing so were twofold: first, the KRG was eager to cultivate close ties with one of its neighbours and Turkey seemed a natural choice, given their historically close ties and mutual loathing of the PKK and its leader, Abdullah Ocalan. Secondly, KRG officials were eager to develop a source of revenue independent of Baghdad to help create the conditions required for its eventual declaration of independence.

Ankara took the KRG's proposal seriously, appreciating the fact that its near-total reliance on oil exports for revenue could strengthen Turkey's position and influence in northern Iraq. However, Ankara's continued preference for the central government in Baghdad meant that it could not, in reality, support the KRG's oil policy, not least because of the ongoing dispute between the KRG and Baghdad about the extraction of oil under the Iraqi constitution. According to Baghdad's interpretation, all oil pumped in Iraq must be sold by Baghdad's Ministry of Oil, which then

---

[62] Ali Khedery, 'Why We Stuck with Maliki – and Lost Iraq', *Washington Post*, 3 July 2014.

[63] Kirk H Sowell, 'Iraqi Election Results Expose Dramatic Shifts in Power', *The National*, 9 June 2014.

transfers 17 per cent of all oil sales to the KRG.[64] The Kurds, by contrast, argue that they have the right to market and sell the oil within their region independently, and then transfer 83 per cent of the profits to accounts controlled by the Ministry of Oil.[65]

Thus, while Ankara prioritised its relationship with Baghdad, between 2005 and 2010, it sought to distance itself from the dispute and instead adopted a cautious policy designed to keep its options open. On the one hand, Ankara allowed two small, Turkish-affiliated oil companies (Genel Energy and Petoil) to begin work in Iraqi Kurdistan. However, on the other, it made clear that it would only take steps to facilitate the independent export of Kurdish oil without Baghdad's approval 'if and when it has become convinced that the situation in Arab Iraq has become so unstable that it threatens its strategic interests'.[66]

It was only once Iraqiya had been sidelined by the Maliki-led government in Baghdad in 2011 that the Turkish government opted to take sides in the Iraqi oil dispute, agreeing in 2012 to facilitate the export of Kurdish oil without Baghdad's consent. This decision coincided with a rapprochement between Barzani and Atheel Al-Nujaifi in Nineveh. With Turkish backing, the two sides made amends, entering into a strategic partnership to counterbalance Shia power in Baghdad.

This change in direction marked a serious departure from Ankara's previous approach to Iraq – and not just to the balance of its support to the various parties and its long-time caution with regard to the KDP in the Kurdistan Regional Government. Between 2003 and 2010, Turkey had advocated a strong and centralised Iraqi government that maintained control over Mosul. By agreeing to export Kurdish oil, Turkey radically reversed course and began to take indirect steps to facilitate the break-up of the Iraqi state. However, the events of 2011 had revealed the limitations of Turkey's influence within Baghdad. Ankara's decision to support the KDP, while maintaining its support for Sunni political groups, thus represented something of a capitulation to Iran, whose dominance in Baghdad had also been underlined.

This shift in policy has had mixed results. On the one hand, the KRG began to export crude oil to Turkey by truck in 2012, before the two sides finished construction of an independent oil pipeline from Iraqi Kurdistan to the Turkish port of Ceyhan in 2014.[67] The KRG now exports oil through

---

[64] Steven Mufson, 'How the U.S. Got Mixed Up in a Fight over Kurdish Oil – With a Unified Iraq at Stake', *Washington Post*, 4 August 2014.

[65] Matthew Phillips, 'A Mysterious Oil Tanker Might Hold the Key to Kurdish Independence', *Bloomberg Business Week*, 23 October 2014.

[66] ICG, 'Iraq and the Kurds: Trouble Along the Trigger Line', Middle East Report No. 88, 8 July 2009.

[67] Brian Swint, 'New Oil Pipeline Boosts Iraqi Kurdistan, the Region Made of Three Northern Provinces', *Washington Post*, 13 June 2014.

the pipeline without the approval of Baghdad. However, in retaliation, Baghdad stopped sending the KRG its allotted 17 per cent of the Iraqi budget. The fact that civil servants in the KRG went without pay for months only served to undermine indirectly Ankara's ally, KRG President Barzani.[68]

Turkey's energy policy has also further undermined its influence with Baghdad – and particularly with the Shia political groups, over which Turkey had only very limited influence in any case. This turn of events has seriously compromised Ankara's long-held intention to carve out a zone of influence that incorporated Iraq, as was first envisioned in Davutoglu's *Strategic Depth*. Turkey's subsequent efforts to play a more prominent role in Iraqi politics have continued to be stymied.

The AKP Sides with Iran: Mediation and *Ostpolitik*

Historically, Turkish–Iranian relations have been undermined by Tehran's support for the PKK and by Turkish concerns about Iran's Islamist leadership.[69] However, as with Syria, relations began to improve after the capture of Ocalan in 1999 and as a consequence of the AKP's focus on improving relations with all of its neighbours after it was elected in 2002. Indeed, the AKP actively sought to improve Turkish relations with Iran in the years immediately after 2002, prioritising the economic elements of the bilateral relationship, whilst also seeking to deepen political and security ties.[70] Since then, unlike the AKP's approach to the Arab world, its Iran policy has stayed relatively consistent, despite the fact that the two sides are at odds over the trajectory of Iraqi politics and, more recently, the civil war in Syria. Thus this section goes beyond the commencement of the Arab upheavals, focusing on Turkish policy towards Iran from the AKP's election in 2002 right up to the present day.

The AKP's Iran policy is premised on assumptions made about geopolitics.[71] Davutoglu has argued that Turkey and Iran both have geopolitical and cultural links with countries in the Middle East, Central Asia and the Caucasus. In *Strategic Depth*, Davutoglu referred to Iran and Turkey as comprising two of the three sides of a regional triangle (the third being Egypt). These three states, he argued, envelop the weaker and artificially created Arab states. In turn, Iran, Turkey and Egypt have influence and links to different areas in the Middle East. Turkey's influence

---

[68] Denise Natali, 'Iraqi Oil Dispute Reveals KRG Vulnerability', *Al-Monitor*, 28 February 2014.
[69] Robert Olson, 'Turkey–Iran Relations, 1997 to 2000: The Kurdish and Islamist Questions', *Third World Quarterly* (Vol. 21, No. 5, August 2010), pp. 871–90.
[70] Omer Taspinar, 'Turkey's Middle East Policies: Between Neo-Ottomanism and Kemalism', Carnegie Endowment for International Peace, 7 October 2008.
[71] Davutoglu, *Stratejik Derinlik*, pp. 433–36.

extends throughout the Anatolian basin and into modern-day Syria and northern Iraq, whereas Iran's extends throughout the Mesopotamian basin into much of southern Iraq.[72] This understanding of geopolitics means that Turkey views itself as being in competition with Iran for influence in contested areas throughout the Middle East, although it also recognises some natural limits to its own influence. Thus the AKP's early attempts to mediate between Hamas and Fatah in Palestine, to engage with Assad in Syria and, from 2005, to play a more prominent role in Iraqi politics were part of a larger endeavour to deepen Turkish influence in the areas that have been defined as being the country's natural hinterland. On the other side of the same coin, Ankara's collective efforts in the region were also aimed at lessening Iranian influence, which the AKP views as a destabilising force.

However, this has not prevented Turkey from co-operating with Iran where it would be beneficial – one such example being borne of the two countries' mutual distrust of Israel. In a show of good faith to Iran, Hakan Fidan, the director of Turkey's intelligence organisation, MIT, reportedly passed US intelligence assessments about the Iranian government to his counterpart in the Islamic Republic in 2010.[73] Fidan is also accused of passing the names of ten Iranians who worked with the Israeli intelligence services in Turkey to Iran – an act reportedly in retaliation for the *Mavi Marmara* incident earlier that year.[74] Such actions are consistent with Davutoglu's understanding of regional affairs and his assertion in 1996 that close ties with Israel undermine Turkey's relations with Iran and its other Arab neighbours, thereby limiting Turkish regional influence.[75]

Such geopolitical considerations have formed only one prong of Turkey's policy towards Iran, however. The second relates to Turkey's energy and economic interests in Iran, which have led the AKP to refuse to publicly support the imposition of unilateral sanctions limiting trade and energy relations with Iran.

Again, this hints at Ankara's willingness to co-operate with Tehran in areas where their specific interests align. With regard to its energy policy, for example, Turkey has historically been highly dependent on Iran for natural gas, and it is currently the destination for more than 90 per cent of Iran's natural-gas exports,[76] which constitute 20 per cent of

---

[72] *Ibid.*, pp. 404–05.

[73] Adam Entous and Joe Parkinson, 'Turkey's Spymaster Plots Own Course on Syria', *Wall Street Journal*, 10 October 2013.

[74] David Ignatius, 'Turkey Blows Israel's Cover for Iranian Spy Ring', *Washington Post*, 16 October 2013.

[75] Davutoglu, 'Turkiye Israil Guvenlik Anlasmasi ve Yeni Dengeler'.

[76] US Energy Information Administration, 'Natural Gas Exports from Iran: A Report Required by Section 505 (a) of the Iran Threat Reduction and Syria Human

Turkey's natural-gas consumption. The AKP blames its near-total reliance on foreign energy for its high current-account deficit, which foreign economists suggest makes the Turkish economy vulnerable to changes in global liquidity.[77] The AKP therefore argues that Western–Iranian tensions have negatively affected the price of energy, exacerbating Turkey's greatest economic weakness. Moreover, the AKP has also worked hard to expand trade links with Iran: Turkish and Iranian officials have set a goal of increasing bilateral trade to $30 billion per year by 2015. Yet, while bilateral trade has increased considerably, from $1 billion in 2001 to close to $15 billion in 2014, much of this is attributable to the increased cost of energy and Turkey's export of gold to Iran to pay for natural gas.[78]

Turkey's reliance on Iran for energy and its emphasis on increasing bilateral trade have inevitably influenced the AKP's approach to sanctions. A number of Turkish political parties, including the AKP, have historically shunned the imposition of sanctions against Iran. These measures decrease Turkish business opportunities in a neighbouring country, whilst also making it more difficult for Ankara to purchase Iranian energy resources. These factors have in turn fed into the AKP's stance on Iran's nuclear programme, which continues to differ from that of the US and Turkey's other Western allies: Ankara argues that the Treaty on the Non-Proliferation of Nuclear Weapons (NPT) guarantees Iran's right to pursue a peaceful nuclear programme. Turkey's policy is based on a number of concerns regarding Western efforts to limit the spread of nuclear technology to emerging nuclear states; indeed, the AKP has an incentive to ensure that concerns over Iran's nuclear programme do not prevent the export of nuclear technology to its neighbours.

However, owing to the assumption that Iran and Turkey are ultimately in competition for influence in the Middle East, the AKP does have its own concerns about Iran's nuclear programme. In response, Ankara has continued the development of Turkish conventional forces, designed to defend against ballistic-missile attack. It has also sought to persuade Tehran to be more forthcoming with the international community about its nuclear history and has asked the country to sign a more intrusive inspection protocol with the International Atomic Energy Agency. These attempts to cajole Iran have been underpinned by Ankara's rejection of the use of unilateral sanctions and coercive rhetoric, based on the argument that they undermine the diplomatic process because they

---

Rights Act of 2012', US Department of Energy, October 2012, <http://www.eia.gov/analysis/requests/ngexports_iran/pdf/full.pdf>, accessed 5 December 2014.

[77] Entous and Parkinson, 'Turkey's Spymaster Plots Own Course on Syria'.

[78] Mehul Srivastava and Isobel Finkel, 'Bling for Minister Mastermind Greased Secret Turkey Gold Trade', *Bloomberg*, 25 June 2014.

help to empower hardliners, rather than moderates who are more willing to come to an agreement on the nuclear issue. Turkey's Iran policy, therefore, blends the development of more capable defences with a continued emphasis on diplomacy.

In line with this, in May 2010, Turkey, Brazil and Iran concluded an agreement known as the Tehran Declaration, which called for the export of 1,200 kg of low-enriched uranium (LEU) to Turkey in exchange for fresh fuel rods for the Tehran Research Reactor (TRR). The P5+1 (the five permanent members of the UN Security Council and Germany) had previously offered Iran a similar proposal, but the deal broke down after Iran demanded that the swap take place simultaneously, on Iranian soil. The Turkish- and Brazilian-brokered fuel swap was also extremely problematic in its demand that the fuel rods for the TRR be delivered within a year of the LEU being handed over, and because it did not account for increases to Iran's larger stockpile of LEU. With neither Turkey nor Brazil able to deliver material to Iran, they had to rely on France for the production of reactor fuel. However, the French providers of the fuel could not possibly have met the deadline in the agreed text, owing to the time needed to develop the reactor-specific fuel – and non-delivery of the fuel rods would give Iran the right to demand the return of the LEU being stored in Turkey. Moreover, the agreement did not address Iran's decision to enrich uranium to 20 per cent purity, at which point it can be further enriched to weapons grade more quickly.[79]

The AKP rejected criticisms of the Tehran Declaration, however, arguing that the agreement with Iran was the first of its kind and a confidence-building measure that was worth pursuing. Meanwhile, in June 2010, Turkey (and Brazil) voted against the US- and European-backed sanctions resolution under consideration by the UN Security Council, despite this undermining its relationship with the US. No doubt the AKP's resentment at the West's and Russia's negative reaction to the Tehran Declaration played some part in this decision.

Shortly thereafter, a high-level AKP delegation visited Iran and proposed deepening economic ties, but these overtures were rejected. Instead, the Iranian representatives indicated that Ankara should thank Tehran for helping to transform Turkey into a global power.[80] This marked the beginning of a precipitous decline in Turkish–Iranian relations. The two sides would subsequently support different political factions in Iraq and ultimately find themselves pursuing radically different policies after the start of the Syrian civil war.

---

[79] Mark Fitzpatrick, 'Containing the Iranian Nuclear Crisis: The Useful Precedent of a Fuel Swap', *Perceptions* (Vol. 16, No. 2, Summer 2011), pp. 35–38.
[80] ICG, 'In Heavy Waters: Iran's Nuclear Program, the Risk of War and Lessons from Turkey', Middle East Report No. 116, 23 February 2012.

Nevertheless, Ankara continued to resist enforcing US- and EU-imposed sanctions and even began to surreptitiously pay for Iranian energy with Turkish lira through a state bank, which Tehran would then use to purchase gold, which was then shipped to Iran.[81] Turkey ended this 'oil-for-gold' scheme once the US closed the loophole in its sanctions regime that allowed for this type of trade.[82] However, it has been granted an exemption by the US to continue to import natural gas from Iran, despite US and EU unilateral sanctions.

The 'oil-for-gold' trade helps to underscore the extent to which Turkish–Iranian relations have been compartmentalised during the AKP's time in power. On the one hand, Turkey continued to import large quantities of Iranian energy, even though this violated the spirit of Western-imposed sanctions. However, Turkey and Iran have also remained involved in numerous proxy wars in different countries in the region – including in Syria, where Ankara and Tehran are still engaged in an intense proxy battle over the future of Assad.

In Iraq, the two countries have worked at cross-purposes since 2005. Furthermore, Turkey's antipathy toward Maliki and his Dawa Party deepened the chasm separating the two powers' political ambitions in the country and throughout the region as a whole. This rivalry extends to Kurdistan: while the two countries share an interest in preventing the establishment of an independent Kurdistan, they both support different proxies and political actors in the KRG, with the AKP seeking to strengthen Barzani's KDP and Iran maintaining links to the PUK and its leader Jalal Talabani.

Indeed, the two sides are at odds in nearly every country experiencing political turmoil. Beyond energy relations and a mutual interest in preventing the formation of an independent Kurdistan, there does not appear to be any major area in which their policies align. Thus, the pragmatic pursuit of stronger trade links notwithstanding, Turkish–Iranian relations have been undermined by the two countries' long-term political goals and conflicting regional interests. It seems likely that they will continue to compete for influence throughout the Gulf and in the Levant for the foreseeable future.

The Calm Before the Storm: Turkey Before the Arab Upheavals

Between 2002 and 2011, the AKP had some notable foreign-policy successes. The most dramatic of these was the increase in trade with Syria and Iran. Ankara's ambitious diplomatic efforts in relation to

---

[81] Jonathan Schanzer and Mark Dubowitz, 'Iran's Turkish Gold Rush', *Foreign Policy*, 26 December 2013.
[82] Asli Kandemir, 'Turkey–Iran Gold Trade Wiped Out by New U.S. Sanctions', *Reuters*, 16 February 2013.

Israel-Palestine question, however, were unsuccessful, owing to the difficulties in the relationship with Jerusalem and Turkey's decision to ally with Hamas. For much of the period from 2002 to 2011, the AKP's foreign policy was defined by its embrace of the status quo. However, its actions were largely guided by its expectation that, eventually, this status quo would be swept away as governments more representative of the masses came to power across the region. Aware that Turkey lacked the capacity to significantly alter the region's political status quo on its own, Ankara instead sought to manoeuvre itself so that it would benefit from the changes that were brewing independently across the Middle East. The AKP, therefore, opted to play the long game and focus on areas that would deepen its influence whilst it prepared for the eventual demise of the Arab world's political order.

However, where states were already undergoing political transitions, as in Iraq and Palestine, Turkey did seek to carve out alliances with like-minded proxies. In Iraq, this policy was tethered to Turkey's distrust of Iran, its views on Kurdish empowerment and, eventually, its problems with Maliki. However, in Palestine, the AKP disavowed its prudent, initial embrace of *ostpolitik* in the mid-2000s in favour of a more ideological policy based on its relations with Hamas – a policy which would increasingly characterise its approach to regional affairs.

Ankara's foreign policy in this period was only loosely based on Davutoglu's concept of strategic depth; but with the onset of the Arab upheavals in late 2010 (as explored in Chapter III), this concept finally came to the fore. The protests that broke out across the region appeared to provide Turkey with the opportunity to establish itself as the region's dominant power – an opportunity that was grasped by the country's recently appointed foreign minister, Ahmet Davutoglu.

III. THE END OF 'ZERO PROBLEMS', 2010–13

The AKP was not prepared for the start of the Arab upheavals in late December 2010. As part of its policy of *ostpolitik*, Ankara had built much of its regional policy around its embrace of the status quo and the development of closer ties with the region's autocrats. Consequently, as events unfolded, Turkey initially reacted cautiously and advocated for cosmetic democratic changes in every country affected except Egypt. However, after it became clear that the AKP-supported leaders would fall, Ankara chose to support the political party with links to the Muslim Brotherhood in Egypt, Tunisia, Libya and Syria. The AKP, in turn, was heralded by many in the West as a potential 'model' for the new crop of religiously conservative political movements poised to take power in these countries in the wake of the upheavals.

In retrospect, it is clear that while Turkey's regional influence reached its zenith in early 2011, it quickly began to fade after the subsequent transformation of the upheavals – and the onset of an anti-Brotherhood backlash in much of the Arab world. The decline of the 'zero problems' approach began in February 2011, after Ankara's policy of support for the Muslim Brotherhood in different Arab polities cast Turkey as a partisan actor and exposed it to backlash from those political elements that did not support the Brotherhood.

Indeed, Ankara's response to the Arab upheavals tied Turkey's foreign policy to the success of one particular political group. This ultimately limited Turkish influence, as the Brotherhood lost its wide-spread appeal and lost ground to forces in the Arab world uncomfortable with the group's synthesis of politics and Islam. Moreover, tension increased between Turkey and the UAE, Jordan and Saudi Arabia – the latter being of particular importance, given its position as the Arab world's most powerful state. Turkey's political fortunes began to suffer as the region's politics moved on after the Arab upheavals and the old and anti-democratic Arab elites pushed back against the empowerment of the Brotherhood.

This chapter briefly details the AKP's domestic consolidation of power, before discussing Turkey's policies shortly before, during and after the tumult in Tunisia, Egypt and Libya.

The AKP's Domestic Strength

The start of the Arab upheavals coincided with a series of domestic developments in Turkey that strengthened the AKP's political power. Between 2009 and 2011, the AKP won three different elections. In the 2009 local election, the AKP won the largest proportion (38.9 per cent) of the vote. Shortly thereafter, the party successfully campaigned for the passage of a series of constitutional amendments in a national referendum in 2010. And in the 2011 national election, the AKP won 49.8 per cent of the vote – which translated into 327 out of a possible 550 seats in parliament. The AKP's impressive electoral victories moved in tandem with domestic efforts to rein in the power of the military. These efforts began in 2002, but were pursued aggressively from 2008, after the military clumsily tried to prevent Abdullah Gul from being nominated as president in view of the fact that his wife wears a headscarf.

The consolidation of the AKP's power via democratic and judicial means prompted outside observers to put forward the notion of a 'Turkish model' of governance after the start of the Arab upheavals in Tunisia in mid-December 2010. The region's parties affiliated with the Muslim Brotherhood embraced this concept and often sought to compare their political aspirations to those of the AKP – even going as far as to adopt party names and political symbols similar to those of Turkey's ruling party. For example, Egypt's Freedom and Justice Party and Libya's Justice and Construction Party bear obvious similarities to the AKP's use of the terms Justice and Development.

While Turkey disavowed references to the Turkish model, the party leadership embraced the idea that the AKP could serve as an 'inspiration' for the states in transition. Davutoglu, for example, heralded the 'Turkish democratic experience' and 'the evolution of civilian–military relations' in the country as proof of the compatibility of democracy with Islam. These experiences, Davutoglu argued, 'could constitute an inspiration for the regional countries under transition',[1] not least 'because Turkey has shown that Islam and democracy can co-exist perfectly'.[2]

---

[1] Republic of Turkey, Ministry of Foreign Affairs, 'Interview by Mr. Ahmet Davutoglu published in AUC Cairo Review (Egypt) on 12 March 2012', <http://www.mfa.gov.tr/interview-by-mr_-ahmet-davutoglu-published-in-auc-cairo-review-_egypt_-on-12-march-2012.en.mfa>, accessed 30 October 2014.

[2] *Agence France Presse*, 'Despite Fallout, Turkey Seeks to "Inspire" Arab Revolt', 16 June 2011.

The rapid changes in the region prompted Ankara to fully incorporate elements of Davutoglu's 2001 book *Strategic Depth* into Turkish foreign policy. This decision did not happen overnight, but was a result of the regional events and the rapid overthrow of three Arab dictators, first in Tunisia.

Change in Tunisia: Ankara Reacts Cautiously

Tunisia had never been a priority for the AKP's foreign policy. In his 2001 book *Strategic Depth*, Davutoglu had criticised the autocratic government and its leader Zine El-Abidine Ben Ali, arguing that Tunisia was one of many states in the Middle East that used post-colonial nationalism to construct a political ideology that was incongruent with the history of the region.[3] In spite of this criticism, the Turkish Ministry of Foreign Affairs chose largely to ignore the protests that broke out in Tunisia in December 2010. Ankara's foreign policy has historically been risk-averse, and in this instance Turkey was initially cautious and followed a policy of non-interference in another state's domestic affairs.

The Foreign Ministry only issued its first statement about the protests on 14 January 2011 – the day Ben Ali resigned from office, and close to a month after the start of the protests. The US, by contrast, had issued its first statement on 8 January – having summoned the Tunisian ambassador in Washington. The Turkish ministry's statement echoed the sentiments of many of Turkey's allies, expressing 'concern and profound sorrow over the incidents occurring in Tunisia', and regrets about the 'tensions in brotherly Tunisia'. Two weeks later, however, Ankara released a second statement embracing democratic change in Tunisia.[4] Turkey's actions during this period were similar to those of its Western allies, underscoring the fact that Ankara's initial policy was at odds with the ideal put forward in *Strategic Depth* and the arguments made about the inevitable changes to the region's political order. This suggests that Ankara – like much of the rest of the international community – was wary of the unknown, having built a relatively successful foreign policy around *ostpolitik*.

After recognising the revolution, Turkey's Tunisia policy was built upon the AKP's relationship with Rachid Ghannouchi, the leader of the Tunisian Muslim Brotherhood-linked Ennahda Movement. In April 2011, some two months after returning to Tunisia from exile, Ghannouchi announced his intention to visit Turkey to meet with then-Prime Minister Erdogan and the leader of the Turkish Islamist Saadet Party, Necmettin

---

[3] Ahmet Davutoglu, *Stratejik Derinlik* (Istanbul: Kure Yayinlari, 2001), p. 368.
[4] Birol Baskan, 'Arabs' Spring, Turks' Autumn', *Washington Review of Turkish and Eurasian Affairs* (June 2012).

Erbakan.[5] Ghannouchi subsequently described Turkey as a potential model for Tunisian Islamists and described the AKP as a 'successful modern Muslim administration'.[6]

Ennahda had historically close ties with Erbakan and political parties linked to his Islamist movement. Indeed, during his long political career, Erbakan and his associates had developed ties with various Islamist political movements across the region, including the Muslim Brotherhood in Egypt and Syria, Algeria's Front Islamique du Salut, as well as Ghannouchi's Islamist movement in Tunisia. These contacts were cultivated through – and indeed further to – Erbakan's alleged membership of the International Islamic People's Command, an umbrella group based in Libya that reportedly included Ghannouchi among other Islamists.[7]

In March 2011, Ghannouchi praised the former Turkish leader, saying, 'In the Arab world in my generation, when [people] talked about the Islamic movement, they talked about Erbakan. When they talked about Erbakan, it is comparable to the way they talked about [Brotherhood founders] Hassan al-Banna and Sayyid Qutb.'[8]

The AKP and Ennahda sought to downplay these historic links; instead, the AKP focused on working with Ennahda within the framework of a coalition government that would pass a new constitution in Tunisia. In October 2011, Ennahda won the most seats in the newly formed national assembly and partnered with the liberal Congress for the Republic and the left-of-centre Ettakatol Party to draft a new constitution.[9]

In March 2012, then-President Gul travelled to Tunisia. During his visit, he addressed the Tunisian assembly, where he compared the protest movements sweeping across the Arab world with the revolutions of Eastern Europe in 1989. In an overt reference to the theories underpinning strategic depth, Gul also referred to the Tunisian revolution as a rebuttal to 'the Orientalist misconception that Islam, democracy, and modernity

---

[5] *Agence France Presse*, 'Tunisia's Opposition Leader to Visit Turkey: Report', 25 February 2011.
[6] *Anadolu Agency*, 'Tunisian Banned Party Leader Ghannouchi to Visit Turkey in March', 25 February 2011.
[7] Philip Robins, *Suits and Uniforms: Turkish Foreign Policy since the End of the Cold War* (London: Hurst & Company, 2003), p. 151. See also 'Groups Issue Statement on Gulf Mediation', Al Sha'b, as published in *Daily Report*, Near East and South Asia, FBIS-NES-90-184, 18 September 1990. See also *Hurriyet Daily News*, 'CHP Deputy Questions Erbakan's Relations with Libyan Leader', 12 May 1997.
[8] *Hurriyet Daily News*, 'Tunisian Islamist Leader Embraces Turkey, Praises Erbakan', 3 March 2011.
[9] *Guardian*, 'Tunisia's Election Winners Form Interim Government after Uprising', 22 November 2011.

cannot find accord'.[10] Similarly, in 2014, Davutoglu, whilst speaking in reference to democracy in the Arab world said, 'there is an Orientalist approach ... In the outside world they say: "these Muslims, they really need an authoritarian leader, it doesn't work any other way" ... This is a form of hidden racism'.[11] Back in 1994, Davutoglu had referred to this as the 'Algeria–Haiti' paradox, whereby Western states argued against the military's intervention in Haitian politics as an affront to democracy, but supported the military's involvement in Algerian politics out of a fear of radical Islam.[12]

Thus, Turkey eventually came to view the Tunisian revolution through the lens of the theories underpinning the policy of strategic depth. Yet, its handling of the subsequent revolutions in Egypt and Libya differed considerably to its relatively hands-off approach to the uprising in Tunisia. In Egypt, Ankara eagerly embraced regime change, whilst in Libya it resisted efforts to help topple Muammar Qadhafi. Ankara's different approaches in these countries help to shed further light on the key drivers of Turkish foreign policy.

Embracing Mubarak's Overthrow: The Origins of Turkey's New Foreign Policy

In contrast to its early approach in Tunisia, Turkey eagerly supported the overthrow of Hosni Mubarak in Egypt. Six days after the Egyptian Revolution began on 25 January 2011, Erdogan postponed a scheduled trip to Cairo and implored Mubarak to 'lend an ear to the people's cries and extremely human demands',[13] adding that 'no government can survive against the will of its people'.[14] The next day, during his weekly address to AKP parliamentarians, Erdogan called on Mubarak to resign, saying, 'For the sake of Egypt, Mr. Mubarak must take the first step. He must do something to instigate change'.[15]

The change in the AKP's rhetoric was likely the result of the evolution of a more coherent Turkish policy on the Arab upheavals, as

---

[10] Presidency of the Republic of Turkey, 'Address by H.E. Abdullah Gül to the Founding Assembly of Tunisia', 8 March 2012, <http://www.tccb.gov.tr/speeches-statements/344/82302/addreb-by-he-abdullah-gul-to-the-founding-abembly-of-tunisia.html>, accessed 30 October 2014.

[11] Jonny Hogg and Nick Tatersall, 'Turkey, Frustrated with West, Clings to Fading Vision for the Middle East', *Reuters*, 1 October 2014.

[12] Ahmet Davutoglu, 'The Clash of Interests: An Explanation of the World [Dis]order', *Intellectual Discourse* (Vol. 2, No. 2, 1994), pp. 122–23.

[13] *Guardian News Blog*, 'Egypt Protests – Tuesday 1 February', 1 February 2011.

[14] Benjamin Harvey, 'Erdogan Tells Egypt's Mubarak He Should Listen to His People', *Bloomberg*, 1 February 2011.

[15] Joe Parkinson, 'Turkey: Mubarak Should Leave Now', *Wall Street Journal*, 2 February 2011.

well as its preference for the ousting of Hosni Mubarak in favour of a Muslim Brotherhood-dominated political system in Egypt. On the challenges involved in defining its approach to the upheavals, Davutoglu wrote in 2013:[16]

> The Arab Spring ... presented us all with difficult decisions: We either could maintain ties with these oppressive rulers, or we could support the popular uprisings to secure basic democratic rights. More significantly, the uprisings also posed a challenge to the conceptual foundations of our new foreign policy, which we had carefully nurtured over the years.

Turkey chose to 'support the popular uprisings to secure basic democratic rights'.[17] However, at the time of the Egyptian uprising in 2011, Ankara's approach was more nuanced and was based on a country-specific understanding of the events unfolding in the Arab world. Turkey had much to gain by supporting the overthrow of Mubarak and the transition to a more democratic system in the country, for several reasons. First, Ankara was sincere in its desire to see democracy spread across the region. Second, the likely election of a Muslim Brotherhood-backed political party would ensure the deepening of Turkish influence in Egypt. Third, Turkish policy-makers were eager to create an Ankara–Cairo axis that would enhance Turkish power along the periphery of the Middle East.

In relation to the latter point, Davutoglu, for example, argues that the region is defined by three concentric geographic triangles. The outermost triangle, as previously stated, includes Egypt, Turkey and Iran. These three outermost states are the most powerful, and the states within the triangle's interior are seen largely as the artificial constructs of European imperialism (with the second triangle including Syria, Iraq and Saudi Arabia, and the innermost triangle including Jordan, Palestine and Lebanon). As explained in the introductory chapter, Davutoglu argued in 2001 in *Strategic Depth* for the expansion of Turkish influence into the coastal states bordering the Mediterranean – creating a zone of influence from Anatolia to Gaza. This conception of geopolitics necessitated close ties with Egypt – a regional power and one corner of Davutoglu's outermost triangle. However, the AKP had faced difficulties cultivating close ties with Mubarak, and thus it viewed the upheaval in Egypt as an opportunity to support a radical change to the political status quo.

The AKP's problems with Mubarak were due to lingering Egyptian suspicions about the AKP's links to the Muslim Brotherhood. These dated back to Mubarak's interaction with Erbakan, and their frequent

---

[16] Ahmet Davutoglu, 'Zero Problems in a New Era: Realpolitik is No Answer to the Challenges Posed by the Arab Spring', *Foreign Policy*, 21 March 2013.
[17] *Ibid.*

disagreements about the Muslim Brotherhood during Erbakan's time as Turkish prime minister, from June 1996 to June 1997. In July 1996, for example, during an official visit to Ankara, Mubarak chided Erbakan for his support for the Muslim Brotherhood.[18] Erbakan, who was then also leader of the RP, dismissed this criticism, choosing instead to offer to mediate between the Egyptian state and the Brotherhood to facilitate the latter's reintegration into Egyptian politics, and counselled his Egyptian counterpart to 'treat [the Brotherhood] well' because the party was 'friends' with the RP. Mubarak criticised the RP's approach and asked that Erbakan 'be more vigilant' and try to realise the extent to which the Muslim Brotherhood 'engaged in violence and terrorism' and refused to accept 'democracy', like Turkey's RP.[19]

As was the case with regard to Tunisia, the AKP saw the Egyptian revolution as similar to the 1989 revolutions in Eastern Europe. Davutoglu had in the past criticised the US and its European allies for their handling of the post-Soviet era in the Middle East, arguing that the Western powers had used Francis Fukuyama's 'End of History' thesis as an 'intellectual vanguard and secular baptismal creed' to 'mobilize the world for the achievement of [Western] strategic planning.'[20] Davutoglu had also lamented the failure of the world's institutions to install democracy in Central Asia, the Balkans and the Caucasus, and indirectly blamed the West for using these institutions to advance its own interests, rather than to support democracy. Davutoglu had used similar arguments in relation to Western decision-making in the Middle East. Turkey has since described the West's policy-making in the wake of the Arab upheavals – particularly after the July 2013 coup in Cairo – as being supportive of an autocracy in order to forward its own interests.

As such, from the early stages of the Egyptian revolution, Turkey sought to signal its support for the uprising. Then-President Gul travelled to Cairo in March 2011, becoming the first foreign leader to visit the country after the overthrow of Mubarak. In September 2011, then-Prime Minister Erdogan also visited Tunisia, Libya and Egypt. In Cairo, Erdogan was greeted by thousands of supporters (many of whom were bussed in for the event by the Muslim Brotherhood). He outlined a new Turkish foreign policy during his speech, centred primarily on the promotion of democracy.[21] His speech was an implicit rebuke of the West and its decades-old policy of allying with Arab dictators. Turkey, by contrast, he

---

[18] Robins, *Suits and Uniforms*, p. 151; *Associated Press*, 'Islamic Leader Returns to Turkish Court to Defend Party', 19 November 1997.
[19] *Daily Report*, 'Egypt: Mubarak's Talks in Turkey Detailed', 19 July 1996.
[20] Davutoglu, 'The Clash of Interests', p. 108.
[21] Saban Kardas, 'Turkey and the Arab Spring: Coming to Terms with Democracy Promotion?', German Marshall Foundation Policy Brief, October 2011.

claimed, was opting to 'stand on the right side of history' and support the transition to democracy, regardless of which political party gained power in the election.[22]

During his visit to Cairo in September 2011, Erdogan said in a live television interview, 'The world is changing to a system where the will of the people will rule. Why should the Europeans and Americans be the only ones that live with dignity? Aren't Egyptians and Somalians [sic] also entitled to a life of dignity?'[23] Similarly, during an interview in 2012, Davutoglu urged the international community to support the democratic process in Egypt, regardless of which political party won the election. Referring specifically to the Muslim Brotherhood-backed Freedom and Justice Party (FJP), Davutoglu publicly argued for non-interference by external actors in Egyptian political affairs, and for the need to permit the democratic process to unfold.[24]

Erdogan's visit, however, also showed the limits of Turkish influence in Egypt. On the one hand, his rhetoric engendered incredible support for Turkey amongst the Egyptian public. According to an opinion poll conducted by the Turkish Economic and Social Studies Foundation, 86 per cent of Egyptians had a favourable opinion of Turkey in 2011.[25] Still, in December 2011, when Gallup asked an open-ended question about which political model Egyptians would consider for their political future, only 11 per cent named Turkey, compared to 22 per cent that listed Saudi Arabia and another 8 per cent the US, whilst over 50 per cent of respondents answered 'none' or simply refused to answer the question.[26]

According to the same data, the revolution had increased ultra-nationalist sentiment in Egypt, as evidenced by the post-revolutionary rejection of international organisations like the International Monetary Fund, as well as US-linked non-governmental organisations.[27] This heightened sense of nationalism, according to Mohamed S Younis, helps

---

[22] In a March 2012 interview with the AUC Cairo Review, Davutoglu reiterated the argument he first posited in 1994, saying, 'the presentation of the Muslim world as a potential enemy has also resulted in encouraging oppressive political tendencies in Muslim countries for the sake of preserving Western interests and thus exempting the Muslim world from enjoying the universality of democratic values'. See Republic of Turkey, Ministry of Foreign Affairs, 'Interview by Mr. Ahmet Davutoglu, published in AUC Cairo Review (Egypt) on 12 March 2012'.

[23] David Kirkpatrick, 'Premier of Turkey Takes Role in Region', *New York Times*, 12 September 2011.

[24] Republic of Turkey, Ministry of Foreign Affairs, 'Interview by Mr. Ahmet Davutoglu, published in AUC Cairo Review (Egypt) on 12 March 2012'.

[25] Mensur Akgun and Sabiha Senyucel Gundogar, 'The Perception of Turkey in the Middle East 2011', Turkish Economic and Social Studies Foundation, 2011.

[26] Mohamed S Younis, 'Turkish Delight: The Feasibility of the "Turkish Model" for Egypt', *Turkish Policy Quarterly* (Vol. 10, No. 4, Winter 2012), p. 109.

[27] *Ibid.*

to explain the criticism Erdogan received after he encouraged the drafting of a secular constitution during his September 2011 visit to Cairo.[28] The backlash came in spite of Erdogan's personal popularity in Egypt, thus suggesting that Egyptians were intent on rejecting any effort by foreign countries – even one as popular as Turkey – to give advice about the country's future political system. The Brotherhood, for example, rejected Erdogan's comments, stating that it was 'not allowed for any non-Egyptian to interfere in our constitution'.[29] Undeterred, Turkey then offered former FJP President Mohammed Morsi a White Paper outlining the path to democracy. However, the party rejected this as well.

These spats were minor, but they foreshadowed the limits of Turkish influence over the FJP – and within the Egyptian public more broadly – during the following years. This is not to suggest that the FJP did not value its relationship with the AKP. Rather, these incidents under-scored the flaws in Turkey's view of its future role in the region. While the FJP may have been religiously conservative, its members were still Egyptian, and looked at efforts to guide political decision-making from abroad with suspicion.[30] This situation points to the continued viability of nationalism as a tool for mobilising voters and furthering political legitimacy, even where religiously conservative political parties are in power. Moreover, it raises the possibility that the AKP's overt support for the FJP was a potential source of weakness that the latter's adversaries could use to cast the party as being under foreign influence.

The AKP, however, viewed this differently, seeing its efforts as part of Turkey's overarching support for the democratic process in the Arab world. In the years following the revolution, the AKP focused on tightening ties with the FJP's leadership. For example, during a November 2012 visit to Egypt, Erdogan signed twenty-seven bilateral agreements and agreed to provide a loan of $2 billion.[31]

This policy had two outcomes. On the one hand, Turkey managed to strengthen ties with the FJP and its supporters. On the other, Ankara's

---

[28] *Ibid.*

[29] Marc Champion and Matt Bradley, 'Islamists Criticize Turkish Premier's "Secular" Remarks', *Wall Street Journal*, 15 September 2011.

[30] Younis argues that: 'Many forget that for most Egyptians, Turkey, while respected as a regional leader and important economic trade partner today, is still viewed from a historic lens in Egypt, as a colonial power that ruled the country under Ottoman rule for nearly four centuries (1517–1914). Much of the anti-colonial ultra-nationalist rhetoric that has taken hold of the country lately could as effectively and quickly take hold against an explicit and public effort by Turkey to present its "lessons" in democracy as a model for Egyptians.' See Younis, 'Turkish Delight', pp. 110–11.

[31] Sam Dagher, Matt Bradley and Charles Levinson, 'New Arab Leaders Scramble to Contain Gaza Conflict', *Wall Street Journal*, 17 November 2012.

dogged support for the group created the justifiable perception that Turkey was taking sides in Egypt. Thus, Turkey was not perceived as an actor standing up for democracy, but as an outside actor pushing a particular agenda via the democratic process. As tensions over the FJP's governance began to grow, the AKP was cast as a partisan actor in an extremely polarised Egypt. Ankara's failure to pursue a more neutral policy therefore meant that its influence did not extend beyond its FJP allies. Thus, as public sentiment began to turn against Morsi, Turkey stood to lose the influence it had carved out with elements of the leadership and bureaucracy in Cairo.

Turkey's reasons for so fervently supporting Mohammed Morsi were twofold. First, Turkish intellectuals with close links to the government were eager to establish a Cairo–Ankara axis. The AKP believed that the overthrow of Mubarak, combined with the election of Morsi, signalled the end of the prevailing regional order. This order, Davutoglu argued, was defined by Western support for 'oppressive political tendencies in Muslim countries for the sake of preserving Western interest', and preventing 'the Muslim world from enjoying the universality of democratic values'.[32] Thus, according to Taha Ozhan, now an adviser to Davutoglu, 'If Turkey and Egypt … could form an axis, they … [would] have taken a step that could deeply influence geopolitics in the whole region'.[33] This axis, Ozhan argued, would challenge the regional status quo that since 1978 had been defined by US support for Israel, and the support of Arab dictators for the US.[34]

Second, and related to this, Davutoglu argued that the 'Western strategic interest in preserving undemocratic political systems ha[d] … caused a deterioration of political legitimacy in the Muslim World'. This deterioration, he argued, had led to increased polarisation between the 'secular elites' and the 'Muslim masses', providing 'the hegemonic powers with a golden opportunity to manipulate these internal conflicts for their own strategic aims'.[35] The AKP viewed the revolution in Egypt as part of a broader transition away from the 'Camp David Order' – describing the status quo of Western support for authoritarian leaders – towards a 'New Middle East', similar to that of the democratic transition that the AKP claims to have overseen in Turkey.[36] This portrayal of events was then

---

[32] Republic of Turkey, Ministry of Foreign Affairs, 'Interview by Mr. Ahmet Davutoglu published in AUC Cairo Review (Egypt) on 12 March 2012'.

[33] Taha Ozhan, '"Egypt Turkey" Axis and the New Middle East Geopolitics', SETA Foundation, 17 November 2012.

[34] *Ibid.*

[35] Davutoglu, 'The Clash of Interests', pp. 122–23.

[36] According to Ozhan, 'The Arab people were quite aware of the reasons behind their suffering and they said that it was not only governments that encroached on their democratic rights, which was reflected in their slogan: "the people demand

linked to the theories underpinning strategic depth and Davutoglu's argument that Arab nationalism was destined to fail and be replaced by governments more representative of the Muslim masses.[37]

These assumptions about the changing regional order resulted in a substantial shift in the AKP's approach to the Middle East as events unfolded across the region. Indeed, after initially adopting a hesitant policy *vis-à-vis* the revolts in Tunisia, the subsequent spread of unrest to Egypt reinforced the perception in Ankara that Davutoglu's predictions about the region were coming true. Thus, in addition to political and religious sympathies for the group, the AKP had an incentive to support democracy and the Muslim Brotherhood. However, little attention was paid to the way in which this support was undermining Ankara's carefully cultivated image as a neutral mediator, or the way in which the AKP's support for the Muslim Brotherhood tainted its relationship with other political parties in Egypt and with other regional states determined to prevent the empowerment of the group.

In parallel, as previously noted, the assumptions made in relation to Egypt began to take on a decidedly anti-Western tinge. Despite the decades-old Turkish alliance with the West, the AKP believed that the US (and to a lesser extent Europe) and Turkey were offering two starkly different visions for the future of the Middle East. The AKP, using language strikingly similar to the arguments made by Davutoglu in the 1990s, began to argue that it was supporting democracy, whilst the West – after the start of the protests that would eventually topple Morsi – appeared to be supporting Arab autocracy. This narrative is in fact at odds with American policy in the region, which was premised on US accommodation of

---

the fall of *the order*". The order here does not simply refer to a single government in isolation from other experiences in the region. It must be understood as a broader term, referring to the established order in the region, and, as dictators in the Arab world fall one after another, the new regional order is in the making.' See Taha Ozhan, 'The Arab Spring and Turkey', SETA Foundation, 15 October 2011.

[37] In an overt reference to this, Davutoglu noted in 2012: 'From our point of view, it was expected; we were aware of the urgent need for change and democratic transformation in the region. As you might remember, in my book *Strategic Depth* (April 2001) I have underlined that the stability and political experience in the Arab states were not based on social legitimacy, and that stability was worthless. Likewise, I have also asserted that the transformation in Arab nationalism and the political legitimacy crises in the Arab world would affect the political leadership structures of those countries. As such, from the early years of the previous decade, we started emphasizing the importance of introducing political and economic reforms and upholding dignity, human rights and freedoms, as well as universal values such as the rule of law, transparency, accountability, and gender equality in the region.' See Republic of Turkey, Ministry of Foreign Affairs, 'Interview by Mr. Ahmet Davutoglu, published in AUC Cairo Review (Egypt) on 12 March 2012'.

Egyptian political outcomes and working with whomever came to power.[38]

In addition, this framing of events contradicts Turkey's own handling of the protests in Tunisia, Libya and Syria, where Ankara (between 2010 and 2011) indirectly supported the maintenance of the autocratic status quo. Nevertheless, the perception that Turkey had adopted a principled stand in support of democracy was deeply felt within the AKP, and has been used subsequently to justify Ankara's continued support for the Muslim Brotherhood after the regional backlash against the group began.

To support the FJP whilst in power, Erdogan is reported to have tasked the director of Turkey's MIT, Hakan Fidan, with providing the regime with intelligence reports and political guidance. According to Turkish newspaper *Taraf*, the AKP provided the FJP with intelligence assessments about the Egyptian military and advised the party to improve public services to deepen support amongst sceptical Egyptians who had nevertheless backed the overthrow of Mubarak. The AKP did so because of concerns about a potential military coup and fears that the Egyptian bureaucracy was not loyal to Morsi.[39] The final meeting, according to *Taraf* and another Turkish newspaper, *Sabah*, took place ten days before Morsi was ousted on 3 July 2013. During that meeting, Fidan is reported to have informed Morsi about the potential coup and advised the FJP to resist attempts to force him from power.[40]

In a sign of just how seriously Turkey took the coup against Morsi, Davutoglu cut short a trip to Asia to return for consultations with AKP leaders in Ankara. Davutoglu subsequently labelled the coup as 'unacceptable' and called for Egypt to schedule early elections.[41] The AKP's deputy spokesperson, Huseyin Celik, tweeted, 'I curse the dirty coup in Egypt. I hope the broad masses who brought Morsi to power will defend their votes, which mean democratic honour'.[42] Erdogan himself responded to the coup on 5 July, saying that 'The West has failed the sincerity test … no offence, but democracy does not accept double

---

[38] E-mail correspondence with Steven Cook, Hasib J Sabbagh Senior Fellow for Middle Eastern Studies at the Council on Foreign Relations, 26 October 2014.

[39] Emre Uslu, 'Hakan Fidan, Mursi'yi mi darbecileri mi bilgilendirdi', *Taraf*, 4 September 2013, <http://www.taraf.com.tr/yazilar/emre-uslu-2/hakan-fidan-mursi-yi-mi-darbecileri-mi/27179/>, accessed 31 October 2014.

[40] *Sabah*, 'MIT Mustesarı Fidan, Mursi'yi uyarmis!', 23 August 2013.

[41] *Associated Press*, 'Turkey Slams Morsi's Military Ouster', 4 July 2013.

[42] *BBC Monitoring Europe – Political*, 'Turkish Ruling Party Urges Egyptian President's Backers to Defend Votes – Daily', 4 July 2013; Daniel Dombey, 'Erdogan Attacks West's Reaction to Morsi's Overthrow', *Financial Times*, 5 July 2013.

standards'.[43] His chagrin stemmed from the US's refusal to label the events a coup, ostensibly because of concerns that the use of the term would make it illegal to continue giving the Egyptian military its annual aid package of $1.3 billion. The AKP viewed the coup as further proof of Western hypocrisy and as a reaffirmation of the West's continued support for the Camp David Order.

Ibrahim Kalin, for example, wrote in Turkish newspaper *Today's Zaman* that, 'While the scale and the circumstances are different, this is reminiscent of the Western position toward the Algerian elections of 1991, when the Islamic Salvation Front won about 50 per cent of the vote in the first-ever multiparty parliamentary elections since Algeria's independence'. Indeed, as Robin Wright, a joint fellow at the US Institute of Peace and the Woodrow Wilson International Center, noted at the time of the Algerian coup in 1992, the 'Western reaction was notable largely for its passivity'.[44]

Kalin then drew a link between Algeria and Hamas in Gaza, arguing that 'The Western reaction wasn't any different in the 2006 Palestinian elections, when … Hamas, another nightmare for the Western-secularist establishment, won a free and fair election in the Palestinian territories'.[45] Moreover, Kalin noted that the situations in Algeria, Gaza and Egypt had all since become incredibly polarised – resulting in violence, which Davutoglu has argued allows the West to manipulate events in line with its own strategic interests.[46] Indeed, these arguments paraphrase Davutoglu's earlier work in *Strategic Depth*, suggesting that the AKP had come to view the Egyptian revolution and the subsequent coup as consistent with the arguments made previously about Western decision-making.

As such, Turkey's overt rebuke of the Western approach was ultimately built upon the idea that Ankara's support for the Muslim Brotherhood was a prudent policy on the basis of Davutoglu's argument that the pre-revolution status quo was untenable. Turkey viewed the Muslim Brotherhood as far more representative of a new and – at least from the AKP's perspective – more democratic Egypt. Erdogan, for example, noted in mid-August 2013, 'I believe these people who believe in martyrdom will one day gain their democratic rights in Egypt. If the West wants to test democracy, they have to understand this … If the

---

[43] *Agence France Presse*, 'Turkey PM Blasts Egypt "Coup" as Enemy of Democracy', 5 July 2012.

[44] Robin Wright, 'Islam, Democracy and the West', *Foreign Affairs* (Vol. 71, No. 3, Summer 1992).

[45] Ibrahim Kalin, 'Egypt's Loss', *Today's Zaman*, 10 July 2013.

[46] *Ibid.*

Western countries do not act honestly on this issue, I believe one day democracy will be questioned in the world.'[47]

Turkey's condemnation of the coup resulted in the Egyptian decision to expel the Turkish ambassador in November 2013. This came after Erdogan stepped up his criticism of new Egyptian leader Abdul Fattah Al-Sisi.[48] Turkey had grown even more disillusioned with the coup after Egyptian forces killed some 1,000 people whilst breaking up two Brotherhood-backed sit-in protests in Rabia Al-Adawiya and Al-Nahda in Cairo in July and August.[49] Just hours after this took place, at a large AKP rally, Erdogan held up four fingers (in reference to the Arabic word *rabia*, which means four in English and is the name of the square where one of the mass killings took place) to express his solidarity with the protesters. On 17 August, furthermore, Erdogan condemned Saudi Arabia and the UAE for their political and financial support to Sisi in the weeks and months after the coup. In reference to the billions of dollars of aid given to the Egyptian government in June 2014, Erdogan said, 'those who give $16 billion to support the coup makers are partners of the coup'.[50]

In May 2014, Kalin echoed Erdogan's criticisms, stating that, 'The el-Sisi regime has the blessings of Western and Gulf countries because it is supposedly helping the world fight against extremist Muslims'.[51] Moreover, in reference to former British Prime Minister Tony Blair's assertion in April 2014 that the coup was 'absolutely necessary [for the] rescue of a nation',[52] Kalin argued that, 'The Islamist bogeyman provides again a convenient pretext for state terrorism, dictatorship, misuse of judicial powers and oppression'.[53] The view is a near-verbatim regurgitation of the argument first made by Davutoglu in the 1990s and has since been linked to a broader effort by the AKP to raise the issue of 'Islamophobia' globally.[54]

This rhetoric has served to embroil Ankara in the emerging anti-Brotherhood conflict in the Middle East – with Saudi Arabia, the UAE,

---

[47] Kadri Gursel, 'Erdogan Veers Away from "Reformed Moderate Islam"', *Al-Monitor*, 23 August 2013; *Milliyet*, 'Dunya demokrasiyi sorgular hale gelir', 16 August 2013.

[48] *Al Jazeera*, 'Egypt Expels Turkey's Ambassador', 23 November 2013.

[49] *Human Rights Watch*, 'Egypt: All According to Plan', 12 August 2014.

[50] *Radikal*, 'Erdogan: Yarın belki Turkiye'yi karistirmak isteyecekler', 17 August 2013, <http://www.radikal.com.tr/politika/erdogan_yarin_belki_turkiyeyi_karistirmak_isteyecekler-1146605>, accessed 31 October 2014.

[51] Ibrahim Kalin, 'Egypt's Predicament', *Daily Sabah*, 6 May 2014.

[52] *The Spectator*, 'Full Text: Tony Blair's Speech on Why the Middle East Matters', 23 April 2014.

[53] Kalin, 'Egypt's Predicament'.

[54] Ali Unal, 'Turkey Demands Sensitivity Towards Islamaphobia', *Daily Sabah*, 8 October 2010.

Bahrain and Israel supporting the coup, and Turkey, Qatar and Tunisia backing Morsi and the FJP. Turkey's position in the wake of the coup also undermined the foreign-policy advances it had made between 2002 and 2011. In particular, as of 2013, Ankara was no longer seen as a neutral mediator capable of talking to all parties in the region, and instead found itself engaged in a series of proxy battles, ostensibly over the future of political Islam, in Syria and Libya.

The overall result has been that Turkey is now viewed as part of a pro-Brotherhood bloc in the region. This has had consequences. Jordan's King Abdullah, for example, included Turkey in his list of a new and radical alliance designed to counter Shia empowerment in post-invasion Iraq.[55] The AKP, he told *The Atlantic*, was part of 'a Muslim Brotherhood crescent developing in Egypt and Turkey'.[56] Moreover, in August 2013, the Abu Dhabi National Energy Company (TAQA) delayed longstanding plans to invest in Turkey's lignite coal sector and to assist with the construction of new power plants. Taner Yildiz, Turkey's energy minister, criticised the decision, saying, 'I wish that Taqa's choices weren't based on political reasons ... It seems like the latest incidents in Egypt and Syria have put Taqa in a position to make choices about its energy investments from its perspective'.[57] In addition, since early 2012, friction over the Muslim Brotherhood has undermined Turkey's efforts in Syria. For instance, Turkey's political disagreements with Saudi Arabia have helped to fracture the Syrian rebels, despite Ankara's best efforts to create a united and cohesive Syrian political and military option. (Turkey's Syria policy will be discussed in detail in Chapter IV.)

As such, it is clear that the backlash over the July 2013 coup in Egypt has severely undermined Ankara's foreign policy in the region. Nevertheless, the AKP continues to argue that it is well positioned to benefit from the inevitable return to electoral politics in Egypt, which suggests that it sees its support for the Muslim Brotherhood as a long-term asset for future Turkish foreign policy. Turkey will likely continue its policy of claiming that the West is against the return of democratic politics to Egypt – a view ultimately based on the assumption that the West benefits from political polarisation in the Middle East. The future therefore portends continued Western–Turkish policy differences in Egypt.

---

[55] Jeffrey Goldberg, 'The Modern King in the Arab Spring', *The Atlantic*, 18 March 2013.
[56] *Ibid.*
[57] April Yee, 'Turkish Energy Minister Fires Back over Taqa Power Project Delay', *The National*, 28 August 2013.

Turkey's Confused Libya Policy

Turkish involvement in Libya predates the election of the AKP and the promulgation of the AKP's foreign policy. After then-Prime Minister Turgut Ozal liberalised the Turkish economy in 1983, Turkish firms were welcomed into Libya. In 1984, for example, Libya was the largest source of construction contracts for Turkish companies.[58] Later, in 1996, then-Prime Minister Erbakan visited Libya as part of a tour of Muslim-majority nations in support of his 'Developing-8' group – a proposal to create a Muslim-majority bloc of nations to rival the EU and institutions like what was then the G7. Despite close Turkish–Libyan ties, during Erbakan's visit to Libya in 1996, Libyan autocrat Muammar Qadhafi chided the Islamist leader for Turkey's defence relationship with Israel, and even advocated the creation of an independent Kurdistan.[59] Qadhafi's words may have been based on his irritation with Erbakan after he chose not to attend a ceremony for his 27th year in power, sending Abdullah Gul – then an RP member of parliament – in his place.

While the mercurial Qadhafi may have embarrassed Erbakan in 1996, his government had previously welcomed increased trade with Turkey. According to Philip Robins, by 1990, Turkish companies had completed contracts worth more than $3 billon in Libya.[60] Moreover, Qadhafi had long supported Erbakan's Islamist movement; in 1989, he was reported to have agreed to provide the movement with a $500,000 cash infusion, after the Turkish government cracked down on the group's finances in the wake of the 1980 military coup.[61]

After the 2002 election, the AKP worked to deepen Turkish–Libyan ties. In 2004, it sought to ease tensions related to Qadhafi's advocacy for an independent Kurdistan on the margins of the 2004 Organization of the Islamic Conference. Moreover, after the US announced the resumption of full diplomatic ties with Libya in May 2006 – followed by the UK's decision to sign a 'Joint Letter of Peace and Security' with the Libyan regime that same year – the AKP sought to incorporate Libya into its broader 'African Opening' initiative, which envisioned the opening of scores of consulates and embassies across the continent. In support of this policy, Erdogan travelled to Tripoli in November 2009. During the visit, he and his Libyan counterparts agreed to waive visa requirements, increase the number of flights between Turkey and Libya, and work towards the conclusion of a

---

[58] Jennifer Noyon, 'Bridge Over Troubled Region', *Washington Quarterly* (Vol. 7, No. 3, Summer 1984), p. 80.
[59] William Hale, *Turkish Foreign Policy Since 1774*, 3rd edition (London: Routledge, 2013), p. 228.
[60] Robins, *Suits and Uniforms*, pp. 210–11.
[61] *Ibid.*, p. 150.

free-trade agreement.[62] Turkey's former minister of economic affairs, Zafer Caglayan, told Turkey's semi-official news wire, Anadolu Agency, that Turkey had assumed $21 billion in projects and announced plans for the holding of joint meetings with Libya's minister of public works once every three months to explore further ways to deepen Turkish–Libyan trade.[63] Just one month later, a Turkish construction firm was selected to build Africa's largest shopping mall in Tripoli.[64] Libya also promised to allow for $125 billion of Turkish investment in the country's construction sector in the near future. In 2009, bilateral trade between the countries had reached $2.2 billion, and continued to grow. Shortly before the Libyan revolution in 2011, Turkish investment projects in Libya stood at $60 billion, according to Ersin Takla, the head of the Turkish–Libya Business Council.[65]

Thus, at the outbreak of the Libyan protests in February 2011, the AKP had numerous financial and economic reasons to resist any major changes to the political status quo. Ankara was eager to maintain its economic relationship with the Qadhafi regime and worried that any political change would result in Turkish firms not receiving the billions of dollars they were owed for services rendered. Ankara was also concerned about the safety of its workers in Libya: when the protests started, there were some 30,000 Turkish workers in Libya.[66] These factors prompted Turkey to resist the adoption of a policy of regime change.

Indeed, while Erdogan soon warned Libya about making 'the mistake of turning a blind eye to the people's demands for democracy and freedoms', it stopped short of calling on the Libyan leader to resign.[67] However, he was quickly criticised domestically for having

---

[62] *BBC Monitoring Europe – Political*, 'Turkish PM Describes Visit to Libya as "Very Productive"', 26 November 2009. According to Kemal Demirciler, the Turkish Ministry of Foreign Affairs' head of Visa Section, 'After the visa waiver was signed with Libya, planes between Libya and Turkey are now full, with two flights a day'. See 'Turkey Drops Visa Requirements for More Countries', diplomatic cable sent from the US embassy in Ankara, Wikileaks, 28 December 2009, <https://cablegatesearch.wikileaks.org/cable.php?id=09ANKARA1841>, accessed 14 November 2014.
[63] *Anadolu Agency*, 'Libya Promises Business Worth Billions of USD, Minister Caglayan', 24 November 2009.
[64] *ANSAmed*, 'Turkish Contractor takes on Largest Mall in Africa', 18 December 2009.
[65] As quoted in Ozlem Tur, 'Economic Relations with the Middle East under the AKP – Trade, Business Community and Reintegration with Neighboring Zones', *Turkish Studies* (Vol. 12, No. 4, Winter 2011), pp. 598–99.
[66] Ismail Duman, 'What is Turkey's Position on Libya?', *World Bulletin*, 12 April 2011.
[67] *Agence France Presse*, 'Turkey Warns Libya against "Mistake" of Ignoring People', 22 February 2011.

accepted a Human Rights Award from Qadhafi in 2010, as well as for his failure to call on the Libyan government to stand down. In response, Erdogan underscored the need to protect Ankara's 'national interests' in Libya.[68]

On 26 February 2011, Erdogan responded to the Western push to sanction Libya by condemning Western decision-making. He argued that sanctions would 'harm the Libyan people' and implied that the world powers were using coercive measures to control Libyan oil. In a speech to parliament, Erdogan called on the international community 'to approach Libya not with concerns about oil but with conscience, justice and universal human values', adding that Turkey was 'fed up' with 'oil wars'.[69] While Erdogan publicly condemned Western policy-making, Davutoglu quietly began to work with the UAE to set up an air-bridge to Libya to deliver humanitarian supplies to those affected by the uprising.[70] Turkey's co-operation with the UAE is noteworthy because, from 2014, the two sides would find themselves on opposite sides of a proxy war in Libya. In addition, the conservative Turkish non-governmental organisation Insan Hak ve Hurriyetleri ve Insani Yardim Vakfi (IHH) sent a ship carrying 682 tons of aid to the city of Benghazi in April to provide humanitarian assistance.[71]

However, Turkey remained sceptical of military intervention. In response to concerns about the number of Turkish workers still in the country, Erdogan indicated that 'discussions about an intervention in Libya or sanctions are worrisome considering the people of Libya and foreigners in country'. He later stated, 'reporters have been asking me whether or not NATO should intervene in Libya. It is such … nonsense. What would NATO do in Libya … We oppose it, such a thing cannot even be discussed.'[72] Davutolgu echoed Erdogan's assertions, saying that Turkey was against intervention because the 'Libyan people were against it'.[73]

Turkey's policy began to change in mid-March 2011, reportedly after a series of protests broke out in eastern Libya against Turkey's relationship with the Qadhafi regime. In response to the growing violence,

---

[68] *Ibid.*

[69] Suzan Fraser, 'Turkey's PM Speaks Out against Libya Sanctions', *Associated Press*, 26 February 2011.

[70] *Times of Malta*, 'Turkey Blasts Move for Libya Sanctions', 26 February 2011.

[71] *Hurriyet Daily News*, 'Turkish IHH Sends 682 Tons of Humanitarian Aid to Libya', 12 April 2011.

[72] *BBC Monitoring Europe – Political*, 'Turkish PM Says NATO Should Not Intervene in Libya', 28 February 2011.

[73] *Deutsche Presse-Agentur*, 'Turkey Opposes Military Intervention in Libya', 3 March 2011. See also Akin Unver, 'Turkey's Position on Libya', Foreign Policy Association Blog, 19 March 2011.

and the increased calls for NATO intervention, Ankara called on Qadhafi to appoint a president who had the backing of the protesters. Erdogan indicated that he had personally called Qadhafi's son, Saif, three times to pressure the Libyan leadership to make concessions to appease the protesters.[74] The Libyan leadership disregarded Turkey's minimal demands, and aimed to implement only cosmetic democratic reforms. Yet after the passing on 17 March 2011 of UN Security Council Resolution 1973, which authorised the use of force to protect civilians, Turkey began to moderate its tone on Allied intervention in Libya.

In response to the resolution, the AKP called for a review of NATO plans for the eventual use of force.[75] It made clear that Turkey would not take part in the air campaign and criticised France's leadership of the coalition, after French warplanes began to attack Libyan targets before an emergency NATO meeting had concluded in Paris.[76] Ankara also sought to portray the intervention as an operation sanctioned by the UN – rather than one undertaken solely by NATO forces – in order to give the impression that Turkey was not acting as part of a Western coalition to attack a Muslim state.[77] Erdogan subsequently blamed Qadhafi for ignoring 'Turkish advice' and chastised the Libyan leader for inviting Western military intervention, before expressing his hope that the air strikes would end quickly.[78]

Ankara's decision-making in relation to Libya underscores the extent to which economic concerns dictated its handling of the crisis. Despite moderating its language, Turkey remained a reluctant participant in the coalition until Qadhafi was toppled and then killed in October 2011. Erdogan appeared to be sincere in his belief that the West's ultimate aim was to control Libyan oil reserves, stating on 23 March that, 'If those who rule Libya leave office as soon as possible, they will make things easier and will not provide an opportunity for others to plunder their country'.[79] Turkey's actions, however, also exposed the limits of its influence, even with its NATO Allies.

---

[74] *Agene France Presse*, 'Turkey PM Urges Kadhafi to Appoint President: Report', 15 March 2011.

[75] *Agence France Presse*, 'Turkey Urges Review of NATO Planning on Libya', 20 March 2011.

[76] David Kirkpatrick, Steven Erlanger and Elisabeth Bumiller, 'Allies Open Air Assault on Qaddafi's Forces in Libya', *New York Times*, 19 March 2011.

[77] *Agence France Presse*, 'Turkey Says Ready to Contribute to Libya Operations', 20 March 2011.

[78] *BBC Monitoring Europe – Political*, 'Turkish PM Criticizes Al-Qadhafi for Not Heeding Turkey's Advice to Step Down', 21 March 2011; *Today's Zaman*, 'PM Erdogan Criticizes Gaddafi, Calls for Swift End to Operation', 21 March 2011.

[79] *Agence France Presse*, 'Turkey Questions "Secret Intentions" in Libya Strike', 23 March 2011.

Indeed, despite its criticism of the intervention, Turkey ultimately allowed a military base in Izmir to be used in support of the mission.[80] The AKP only did so, however, once it was presented with a diplomatic *fait accompli*, whereby the US, the UK and France were in favour of the NATO-backed operation, which then left the AKP with little choice but to reverse course, acquiesce to Western pressure and support a mission that it had deep reservations about. At the time of the intervention, NATO had reached a consensus on the need to use military force and had secured support from key Arab states, which eventually forced Turkey to change policies and participate in the mission, albeit in a limited capacity. After recognising that regime change was inevitable, Ankara began working closely with its allies on the ground. In doing so, it relied heavily on Qatar, which also shared political sympathies with the Muslim Brotherhood.

In September 2011, Davutoglu travelled to Paris, where he met with other members of the 'Friends of Libya' coalition. This group was working with Abdel Jalil, the head of Libya's National Transition Council (NTC), which was formed in February 2011 and governed Libya after Qadhafi's removal.[81] Ankara announced on 2 September that it would reopen its embassy in Tripoli and provide the NTC with $300 million in cash, loans and other aid.[82] Moreover, as part of his tour of the states which had been affected by the Arab upheavals, Erdogan and a number of Turkish ministers visited Libya for meetings. Erdogan spoke on 16 September in Tripoli's Martyr's Square, after visiting both Tunis and Cairo. During his speech, he lauded the Libyan resistance and expressed his support for Libya moving forward.

Turkey, along with the UK, Italy and the US, also agreed to train the new Libyan army.[83] The first troops arrived in Turkey in December 2013 for training at a military base near the city of Isparta.[84] However, according to Frederic Wehrey, the collective results of these efforts 'produced dismal

---

[80] According to NATO, 'The operation was commanded by Lieutenant General Charles Bouchard from CJTF Naples, Italy. All NATO air assets participating in Operation UNIFIED PROTECTOR were under the command of Lt Gen Ralph J Jodice, CFAC Izmir, Turkey. Real-time tactical control was exercised by NATO's Combined Air Operations Centre (CAOC) in Poggio Renatico, Italy.' See NATO, 'NATO Arms Embargo and No Fly Zone Implementation for Operation Unified Protector', <http://www.jfcnaples.nato.int/Unified_Protector/AC-IZMIR.aspx?>, accessed 3 November 2014.

[81] *Qatar News Agency*, 'FM Davutoglu Arrives in Paris for Libya Conference', 1 September 2011.

[82] *Reuters*, 'Turkey Says Reopening Embassy in Libya', 2 September 2011.

[83] Frederic Wehrey, 'Modest Mission?', *Foreign Affairs*, 4 November 2013.

[84] *Today's Zaman*, 'Libyan Soldiers Arrive in Turkey for Training', 8 December 2013.

results'. In Turkey specifically, Wehrey notes that, 'attrition rates were high due to poor vetting.'[85]

On the political side, the AKP and Qatar worked closely with the Muslim Brotherhood-affiliated Justice and Construction Party (JCP), established in November 2011 at a party congress in Benghazi.[86] The Brotherhood decided at the congress to form a political party whereby membership would be kept separate from the broader organisation. The JCP modelled itself on Egypt's FJP; its leader, Mohamed Sawan, has also compared his party's political ideology to that of the AKP.[87]

As with the FJP, Turkey's decision to back the JCP proved short-sighted and, once again, limited its involvement to one specific entity. However, unlike in the case of Egypt, the decision ultimately resulted in Turkey and Qatar backing armed rebel militias, battling against groups allied with other regional states like the UAE, Egypt and Saudi Arabia.

Indeed, after the euphoria of the Libyan revolution receded, the new government quickly became consumed by political infighting, augmented by the use of private militias to help secure individual interests throughout the country. The return to violence was of major consequence for Turkey, linked as it was to the JCP failing to garner high levels of political support. As Mary Fitzgerald notes, 'the Brotherhood connection appears to limit the JCP's appeal: Muammar al-Qaddafi's long suppression and demonization of the movement has left many Libyans sceptical of it, while the Brotherhood's setbacks across the Middle East have emboldened Libyan anti-Brotherhood activists'.[88] These setbacks began in Egypt in July 2013 and extended to Libya shortly thereafter. After the overthrow of Morsi, for example, Fitzgerald notes, 'Some within the country's hollowed-out military, along with anti-Islamist activists and militias, make no secret of their wish to see a similar scenario unfold in Libya'.[89]

To be fair, no outside power had much hope of navigating Libya's dizzyingly complex political landscape after the revolution. However, Ankara's policy towards the Arab upheavals irritated other Gulf States, contributing to broader opposition to the JCP. After the coup, Egypt, working with the UAE and other anti-Brotherhood Gulf States, began to support an alliance of individual tribes and militias battling against Islamist

---

[85] Frederic Wehrey, 'What's Behind Libya's Spiraling Violence?', *Washington Post*, 28 July 2014.

[86] *Al Arabiya News*, 'Libya's Muslim Brotherhood Holds their First Congress in Benghazi after 25 Years', 18 November 2011.

[87] Project on Middle East Democracy, 'POMED Backgrounder: Previewing Libya's Elections', 5 July 2012.

[88] Mary Fitzgerald, 'Libya's Muslim Brotherhood Struggles to Grow', *Foreign Policy*, 1 May 2014.

[89] *Ibid.*

forces, known as Libya Dignity. With Turkey and Qatar having reported links to Islamist-allied militias, known collectively as the Libya Dawn coalition,[90] Ankara thus became entangled in a proxy battle that has pitted it against the majority of the Gulf States.

In addition, Turkey's alleged support for Libya Dawn has involved Ankara in a proxy war against former General Khalifa Haftar,[91] who launched and continues to lead Libya Dignity and is supported by the UAE, Egypt and Saudi Arabia. Haftar has made clear that he intends to rout and outlaw the Muslim Brotherhood.[92] To this end, in June 2014, Haftar accused Turkey and Qatar of supporting 'terror' and called on the 'citizens of Turkey and Qatar [to] leave Libya within 48 hours' of his saying so.[93] The AKP denies these links, arguing that it supports national reconciliation and that it is working with all parties to promote political dialogue.

Two months after Haftar's accusations, in August, Emirati pilots, operating out of an airbase in Egypt, struck Libya Dawn militias as they battled rivals in Tripoli. Despite the airstrikes, however, Libya Dawn took over Tripoli, forcing Libya's government, then headed by Abdullah Al-Thinni, to flee the capital and govern from the eastern city of Tobruk. In Tripoli, Libya Dawn asked a failed Islamist prime ministerial candidate, Omar Al-Hassi to form and lead a new government. To date, no foreign government has recognised Hassi's government, instead viewing Thinni as Libya's legitimate ruler.

However, in late October 2014, Turkey's special envoy to Libya, Emrullah Isler, met publicly with Hassi's self-declared government in Tripoli;[94] no other country has yet done so. Just two days before the meeting, Isler also announced that Turkish Airlines would resume flights to the city of Misrata, after clashes resulted in the halting of all international flights to and from the city.[95] Misrata's militias make up the largest component of Libya Dawn, but they reject the Islamist label. Nevertheless, these militias have allied with other Islamist groups, and have been subjected to Emirati air strikes in support of Haftar's forces against militias allied with Libya Dawn near Tripoli.[96]

---

[90] David Kirkpatrick and Eric Schmitt, 'Arab Nations Strike in Libya, Surprising US', *New York Times*, 25 August 2014.
[91] Mary Fitzgerald, 'Libyan Renegade General Khalifa Haftar Claims He is Winning His War', *Guardian*, 24 June 2014.
[92] *Ibid.*
[93] *Reuters*, 'Renegade General Urges Turks, Qataris to Leave East Libya', 22 June 2014.
[94] Ulf Laesing and Ahmed Elumami, 'Rival Libyan PM Meets Turkish Envoy in First Known Meeting with Foreign Visitor', *Reuters*, 21 October 2014.
[95] Heba Al-Shibani and Feras Bosalum, 'Forces from Libyan City of Misrata Say They Seized Tripoli Airport', *Reuters*, 23 August 2014.
[96] E-mail correspondence, Mary Fitzgerald, 26 October 2014.

Turkey has also been accused of having links to Ansar Al-Sharia (ASL) – a jihadist organisation based in Benghazi that has been blamed for the 2012 attack on the US consulate in the city.[97] These reported ties prompted one unnamed American official to state, 'Washington believes Turkey is partnering with Qatar in providing support to Islamist factions and militias in Libya'.[98] Turkey denies these allegations, but in January 2014, members of ASL flew to Turkey to oversee the delivery of aid to the Syrian towns of Salma and Kasab.[99] The boxes used to deliver the aid were stamped with ASL's logo and were delivered – in three separate batches, over a five-day period – by men openly brandishing their ASL links by wearing logo-stamped jackets and shirts.[100]

The decision to allow ASL into Turkey raises a number of troubling questions about the AKP's decision-making, particularly when combined with Turkey's support for the Al-Qa'ida affiliate Jabhat Al-Nusra in Syria. The AKP rejects any links to these groups, but there is no denying that for five days in January 2014 ASL did operate from Turkey. In turn, this raises questions about whether or not Turkey has used these groups to advance its own interests – which are linked to the success of the Muslim Brotherhood – in Syria and Libya.

Recent political developments in Libya and the broader region have pit most of the Gulf States against Turkey and Qatar – a situation that has resulted in the use of military force in Libya and the provision of external support for different political parties and allied proxies in numerous other countries. The current political status quo in the region is now at odds with the view that the AKP's foreign policy had resulted in Turkey having 'an image as a responsible state, which provides order and security to the region, one that prioritizes democracy and liberties, while dealing

---

[97] Aaron Zelin, 'Know Your Ansar Al-Sharia', *Foreign Policy*, 21 September 2012.

[98] Jonny Hogg, 'Turkey's US Relations Show Strain as Washington's Patience Wears Thin', *Reuters*, 23 October 2014.

[99] Aaron Zelin, 'When Jihadists Learn How to Help', *Washington Post*, 7 May 2014. In February 2014, these areas came under attack by groups linked to the Islamic Front – an umbrella group of Syrian rebels that received support from Turkey – and Al-Qa'ida-linked Jabhat Al-Nusra. During the assault on Kasab, numerous reports emerged suggesting that Turkey allowed Jabhat Al-Nusra (which is not a member of the Islamic Front, but co-operates with some Islamic Front groups) and other fighters to transit its territory to attack the town. In April 2014, Ruth Sherlock wrote: 'Turkish authorities gave rebel groups the mandate they needed to attack, allowing them access through a heavily militarised Turkish border post, whose location was strategically vital to the success of the assault … Two days later Kasab was in the hands of an alliance of Islamist groups, including the jihadist Jabhat al-Nusra, aligned with al-Qaeda … [In a]lmost all of the villages approximately 2,000 inhabitants had fled.' See Ruth Sherlock, 'Turkey "Aided Islamist Fighters" in Attack on Syrian Town', *Daily Telegraph*, 14 April 2014.

[100] Aaron Zelin, 'When Jihadists Learn How to Help', *Washington Post*, 7 May 2014.

competently with security problems at home.'[101] Since the start of the Arab upheavals, a combination of an increasingly polarised region and Ankara's foreign-policy missteps have led to the portrayal of Turkey as a sectarian actor operating in favour of the Muslim Brotherhood. These tensions have played out in Libya, but have also resulted in disagreements about Turkey's approach to the Syrian crisis, as well as questions over its future role in the region.

Turkish Isolation

After the overthrow of Ben Ali in Tunisia and Mubarak in Egypt, Turkey was portrayed as a potential model for the Arab countries in transition. The focus on the idea of a 'Turkish model', however, has distracted from Ankara's rather self-interested and uneven policies during the upheavals. Turkey's handling of Egypt differed considerably from its approach to Tunisia, which in turn was very distinct from its handling of the situation in Libya. In Tunisia, a cautious AKP was unsure of how to act, and only embraced regime change after it become clear that Ben Ali was certain to fall from power. In Libya, by contrast, the AKP prioritised its economic interests and chose to disregard the demands of first the protesters and then the rebels with the outset of the conflict. The AKP's policy towards the Arab upheavals therefore cannot be described as an effort to promote democracy or to stand by the people against state oppression. Instead, it has been far more nuanced, based on assumptions made about a changing regional order and how the upending of the Arab world's political status quo would benefit the AKP.

Egypt was the exception to this rule. There, Turkey eagerly embraced regime change because of the AKP's cool relationship with Mubarak and its belief that the installation of a like-minded political party would help to advance its regional interests, including the undoing of what intellectuals close to the party defined as the Camp David Order. The AKP's fervent support for Morsi has since embroiled Turkey in numerous political proxy battles throughout the region. Moreover, it has seriously damaged its relationship with Saudi Arabia, the UAE and Jordan, without having amounted to much in return. Turkey's preferred party in Egypt, the FJP, has been overthrown and, with Morsi in prison, Sisi appears to be firmly in power.

Still, Turkey has been dismissive of the damage its Egypt policy has done to its foreign policy, instead embracing the idea that it stands to benefit in the long term, once the region inevitably returns to electoral politics in Egypt and the pressure for political change begins anew in

---

[101] Ahmet Davutoglu, 'Turkey's Foreign Policy Vision: An Assessment of 2007', *Insight Turkey* (Vol. 10, No. 1, 2008), p. 83.

countries throughout the Middle East. This perspective is based on three assumptions. First, the belief that the 'era of nationalism' will come to an end in the Middle East and a new crop of religiously conservative leaders will emerge, bringing an end to the existing Arab order. Second, the belief that these new religiously conservative leaders will look to Turkey – and more specifically, to the AKP – as a source of political inspiration. Third, the belief that wider religious conservatism will allow Turkey to expand its influence through a shared religious identity with like-minded states.

The interrelated events of the Arab upheavals, however, have combined to thwart Turkey's ambitions in this regard. In contrast to its previous position of influence in the region's post-revolutionary states, Ankara now finds itself embroiled in a proxy war in Libya, sidelined in Cairo, and unwelcome in Riyadh and Abu Dhabi. Indeed, even in Tunisia, which has been lauded as a model for democratic transition in the Arab world,[102] the AKP's preferred party, Ennahda, came in second – winning sixty-seven seats, compared to eighty for the secularist Nidaa Tounes – in an election held in October 2014.[103]

These Muslim Brotherhood-specific problems come on top of Ankara's tensions with Israel, as well as its troubles with Iraqi Shia in Baghdad. Moreover, this rapid decline has taken place in a span of just three years, upending what had been a very ambitious foreign policy up until 2010. These problems have also moved in parallel with the AKP's policies in Syria, which have also contributed to the rapid decline in Turkish influence. In retrospect, the era of the AKP serving as an 'inspiration' was relatively short and led to the party's regional isolation. This isolation has since complicated Turkish foreign policy further, as officials have sought to navigate one of the most vexing political crises in Turkey's history: the Syrian civil war.

---

[102] *Washington Post*, 'Tunisia's Democratic Compromises Should Serve as a Regional Model', 10 January 2014.
[103] Eileen Byrne, 'Tunisia's Islamist Party Ennahda Accepts Defeat in Elections', *Guardian*, 27 October 2014.

IV. STUMBLING IN IRAQ AND SYRIA, 2011-14

The spread of the Arab upheavals to Syria posed a unique set of problems for Turkey's ruling Justice and Development Party (AKP). Despite Ankara's tepid embrace of political change in Libya, then-Prime Minister Recep Tayyip Erdogan tried to capitalise on the changes sweeping through the Arab world. The AKP abandoned its policy of *ostpolitik* in relation to Egypt, while in Tunisia and Libya the party moved on from its early missteps and was eagerly working with Brotherhood-affiliated political parties. Domestically, the idea of a resurgent Turkey in the Middle East bolstered the AKP's popularity and contributed to a growing perception amongst the party's base that Erdogan was a statesman capable of deftly managing global crises. Furthermore, the AKP viewed the protests across the region as a vindication of the party's geopolitical worldview, heralding a changing regional order.

Despite this wider optimism, Turkey viewed the unfolding events in its southern neighbour Syria with trepidation. In 2007, Ahmet Davutoglu described Turkey's Syria policy as a 'striking example' of the success of the 'zero problems with neighbours' foreign policy.[1] Turkey embraced Syrian President Basher Al-Assad, despite Davutoglu's contention, in 2001, that Ba'athist rule in the country had lost its legitimacy following both the end of the Cold War and the death of President Hafez Al-Assad.[2] Indeed, despite the arguments against Ba'athism, the AKP reasoned that close relations with Syria were critical to Turkish foreign policy and the advance of Turkish influence in a region dubbed its 'natural hinterland'.

The unrest in Syria in the spring and summer of 2011 was thus a crucial test for the AKP's foreign policy and for its hitherto growing regional clout. Until September 2011, despite the intensifying violence in Syria, the AKP maintained a policy of support for Assad, shunning the idea

---

[1] Ahmet Davutoglu, 'Turkey's Foreign Policy Vision: An Assessment of 2007', *Insight Turkey* (Vol. 10, No. 1, 2008), p. 80.
[2] Ahmet Davutoglu, *Stratejik Derinlik* (Istanbul: Kure Yayinlari, 2001), p. 372.

of external intervention and instead working to convince the Syrian leader to make cosmetic democratic reforms.

However, despite the AKP's considerable attention to the issue, Assad resisted this pressure to reform and ultimately sided with Iran – a country viewed by Ankara as a competitor for influence within the Middle East. Indeed, Assad came to rely on Iranian military advisers quite heavily following the militarisation of the state response to the protests.[3] Assad's actions were a blow to Turkish prestige, which had hitherto rested on the AKP's argument that the foreign policy it had pursued since coming to power had increased its influence over Syria and Turkey's other Arab neighbours.[4]

In September 2011, Ankara severed ties with the Assad regime, prompted in large part by the increase in violence, and shortly thereafter Turkey prioritised the organisation of an effective Syrian opposition and the provision of support to various Syrian rebel groups. Turkey's continued preference for the Muslim Brotherhood, however, detracted from these efforts. Moreover, Ankara's decision to support certain radical rebel groups, in its determination to remove Assad, placed it at odds with its ostensible allies in the conflict: the West and a number of Arab countries.

The chaos in Syria has resulted in a number of acute security challenges for Turkish policy-makers. The early successes of the Turkish-backed rebels across Syria resulted in the redeployment of Syrian forces from the country's Kurdish-majority areas, which are non-contiguous and situated along Syria's border with Turkey. This allowed the Democratic Union Party (PYD) – linked with Turkey's Kurdistan Workers' Party (PKK) – to gain de facto autonomy over the areas. While the AKP certainly supported the rebel gains, it opposed the PYD's empowerment and subsequently took steps to isolate the group, which have so far failed to prevent the PYD from moving towards its goal of autonomy. Ankara initially assumed that Assad would be forced from power within six months; thus policy-makers were ill-prepared for the PYD's gains in 2011 and 2012.

Moreover, the spread of conflict from Syria to Iraq has resulted in a Western military intervention focused solely on the militant group known as the Islamic State (IS). Turkey's preferred policy of regime change in Syria has been cast aside by its NATO Allies, with the US, other Western countries and a number of Arab partners now implementing an air campaign to 'degrade and defeat' one specific Syrian rebel group. These events have exposed the limits of Turkish power and have resulted in

---

[3] *Al Arabiya*, 'Report: Iranian "Military Advisors" in Syria Seen in Online Footage', 16 September 2013.
[4] Bulent Aras and Rabia Karakaya Polat, 'Turkey and the Middle East: Frontiers of the New Geographic Imagination', *Australian Journal of International Affairs* (Vol. 61, No. 4, December 2007).

Ankara's international isolation. More broadly, Turkey's difficulties in both Syria and Iraq undercut its assumed position as a regional leader and undermined many of the arguments that the AKP had made about its role in overseeing the creation of a new regional order.

Managing the Syrian Problem: Demanding Reforms

Following the outbreak of protests in Tunisia in December 2010, Assad became acutely aware of the dangers posed by the spread of the revolts throughout the Arab world. To help quell the likelihood of major street protests in Syria, his first action was to cancel planned austerity measures and to issue a vaguely worded pledge of reform. By contrast, Ankara largely ignored the events in Tunisia at first; however, by the end of January 2011, it had settled on its policy response. That response (as detailed in Chapter III) was based on support for the overthrow of Egyptian President Hosni Mubarak, while also resisting change in Libya. Then, as the first protests began in Syria in March 2011, Ankara adopted a business-as-usual policy, albeit while prodding Assad behind closed doors to make reforms.[5]

The further spread of the protests in March and the Assad regime's use of force in the southern Syrian city of Deraa did little to change Turkey's approach to the unfolding events, which can be partly explained by Ankara's fears over Kurdish empowerment. The spread of the protests to the Kurdish-majority city of Qamishli[6] – which shares a border and many cultural and familial links with Kurds from Turkey's Mardin Province – prompted concerns about an uprising similar to the 2004 riots throughout the predominantly Kurdish Jazira region in northeastern Syria.[7] A pressing priority for Ankara was the maintenance of a strong and centralised Syrian state so as to prevent the emergence of a Kurdish autonomous zone along the Turkish-Syrian border – and this remained the priority even after Ankara severed ties with Assad's regime in November 2011.

The escalation of violence at the end of March 2011 prompted Erdogan publicly to call on Assad to make political and economic reforms that would address the demands of the protesters. In early April, Erdogan announced that he had spoken to Assad twice since the protests began and he indicated that he would increase his efforts to convince the Syrian leader to make the necessary reforms.[8] On 6 April, Davutoglu, acting as

---

[5] *Agence France Presse*, 'Turkey Scrambles to Cajole Syria into Reform', 27 April 2011.
[6] Nicholas Blanford, 'Syria Protests Escalate, but Could Revolt Really Take Root?', *Christian Science Monitor*, 20 March 2011.
[7] Human Rights Watch, *Group Denial: Repression of Kurdish Political and Cultural Rights in Syria* (New York, NY: Human Rights Watch, November 2009).
[8] Simon Cameron-Moore, 'Turkey to Press Syria on Reforms', *Sunday Herald*, 3 April 2011.

the Turkish president's personal envoy, met with Assad in Damascus to seek his acquiescence to Erdogan's public calls for Damascus to 'positively respond' to the calls for reforms, in order to 'overcome the problems more easily'.[9] However, just days after Davutoglu's visit, Syrian security forces killed some eighty people, prompting the Turkish Ministry of Foreign Affairs to express 'deep concern' and to repeat Erdogan's demand for reforms.[10] Erdogan, meanwhile, again called on Assad directly to oversee the necessary reforms and announced his intention to send Davutoglu back to Damascus for further discussions.[11]

According to *Hurriyet*, a Turkish daily newspaper, the AKP's concerns about the stability of the Assad regime grew more acute after the government began to use force against the protesters. This was partly because Ankara was concerned about the potential for the mass flow of refugees to Turkey in the event of a civil conflict, but it also feared a repeat of the Libyan intervention, which, initiated in March 2011, had ultimately 'allowed some countries to change the regime in Libya, something the United Nations resolutions did not impose'.[12]

These concerns framed Ankara's evolving Syrian policy. Unlike its response to the Egyptian crisis, Ankara's initial preference in the case of Syria was for the regime to reform and remain in power. Indeed, Turkey had an economic and geopolitical interest in maintaining ties with Assad and, as with Libya, resisted the notion of foreign intervention in the conflict. Moreover, there were concerns that the start of a civil conflict could result in the creation of autonomous PKK-allied territories in Syria's Kurdish-majority areas of Afrin, Kobane and Jazira.[13] In this instance, Turkey's policies overlapped with those of its Arab neighbours, many of which were eager for the spread of the revolutions to be halted. To this end, in late April, Erdogan dispatched Hakan Fidan, the director of Turkey's National Intelligence Organization (MIT), to implore the Syrian leader to make the necessary reforms and to end the bloody crackdown on Syrian civilians.[14] However, Assad ignored Turkey's advice, and this inability to sway him at this stage provided an early indicator of the limited

---

[9] *Agence France Presse*, 'Ankara Sends Minister to Protest-Hit Damascus', 6 April 2011.
[10] *Agence France Presse*, 'Turkey Voices "Deep Concern" over Syria Bloodshed', 26 April 2011.
[11] *Agence France Presse*, 'Turkey PM Calls Assad to Press for Reform: Report', 26 April 2011.
[12] *BBC Monitoring Europe – Political*, 'Turkish Daily Says Ankara on Alert over Escalating Tension in Syria', 26 April 2011.
[13] *Agence France Presse*, 'Turkey Scrambles to Cajole Syria into Reform'; Jonathan Head, 'Turkiye'nin Suriye siyasetindeki zor tercihler', *BBC Turkce*, 20 June 2011.
[14] Ivan Watson and Yesim Comert, 'Bloody Syrian Conflict Embarrasses Turkish Allies', *CNN International*, 29 April 2011.

nature of Ankara's actual influence over the Syrian regime, despite its longstanding efforts to cultivate the relationship.

By June 2011, a second element of Turkey's policy had become apparent. The AKP's earlier efforts, prior to the uprising, to mediate between the Assad regime and the Syrian Muslim Brotherhood had been unsuccessful, but it is clear that the party saw the revolution as an opportunity to convince the Assad government to lift the ban on the Brotherhood.[15] As part of its demands for reform, therefore, Turkey is reported to have received a verbal guarantee from Assad to allow the Syrian Muslim Brotherhood to return from exile.[16] Turkey's advocacy of the Muslim Brotherhood in Syria, as throughout the region, was underpinned by Davutoglu's views on both the sources of political legitimacy in the Muslim-majority Middle East and the necessity of bringing the concepts of *Tawhid* and *Tanzih* to the forefront of electoral politics in the region. While Ankara did not yet embrace the Brotherhood's calls for Assad to step down, therefore, it did seek the middle ground by supporting the group's efforts to gain a semblance of power in Syrian politics, and in doing so it took steps towards bringing these concepts to the heart of Syrian governance.

August 2011 once again saw the Turkish government publicly call on its Syrian counterpart to enact reforms following the latter's attack on the Syrian city of Hama (a highly symbolic city, owing to the 1982 Muslim Brotherhood-backed uprising that was forcefully put down by Hafez Al-Assad). Erdogan also publicly expressed his personal outrage and exasperation, warning that, 'Until today, we have been very patient, wondering many times whether we can solve this, whether words translated into actions … But now we have come to the last moments of our patience'.[17] He called on Assad to 'stop all kinds of violence and bloodshed' within fifteen days.[18]

Davutoglu was again dispatched to Damascus but this time he is believed to have suggested that Syria make cosmetic democratic reforms – something Turkey had previously tried to persuade Qadhafi to do in Libya. The reforms demanded would not have resulted in any major changes to the Syrian political structure. Yet these efforts failed, exposing the limits of the country's influence over its neighbour. Indeed, despite the AKP's efforts

---

[15] Carnegie Endowment for International Peace, 'The Muslim Brotherhood in Syria', <http://carnegieendowment.org/syriaincrisis/?fa=48370>, accessed 12 December 2014.
[16] Asli Ilgit and Rochelle Davis, 'The Many Roles of Turkey in the Syrian Crisis', Middle East Research and Information Project, 28 January 2013.
[17] Thomas Seibert, 'Turkey Losing Patience with Syria', *The National*, 8 August 2011.
[18] Alex Christie-Miller, 'Turkey Warns Assad to End the Killing as Tanks Attack Border Towns', *The Times*, 11 August 2011.

since it came to power in 2002, Assad never trusted Ankara, according to Bassam Barabandi, a former Syrian diplomat;[19] he instead began to rely on Iran and Hizbullah once the fighting began to escalate, with the former advising Assad against making any political compromises along the lines proposed by Ankara from the start of the uprising.[20] Damascus' decision to ally with Iran is not all that surprising given Syria's historical alliance with the Islamic Republic, but it came as a surprise to many in Ankara who had come to believe that their growing trade and cultural ties over the previous eight years had resulted in increased political leverage.

Turkey Embraces Regime Change in Syria

Turkey downgraded its ties with the Assad regime in September 2011, albeit while continuing to pressure the Syrian president to enact reforms. In October, however, after a joint Russian and Chinese veto prevented the UN Security Council from authorising sanctions against Assad, Erdogan announced that Turkey would impose unilateral sanctions – and that it would hold large military exercises on the Turkish-Syrian border to try to coerce him into taking these demands more seriously.[21] During the same month, the AKP began to take a more active role in the creation of the Syrian opposition, initially working closely with Qatar to do so. In a significant departure from typical AKP foreign policy, having shied away from sanctions in relation to both Iran and Libya, Turkey joined its allies in the West and the Gulf in imposing sanctions against Assad in late November 2011. Moreover, the passage of these coercive measures marked the end of Turkey's preference for diplomacy in favour of a new policy of regime change.

To hasten Assad's fall, Turkey adopted a three-pronged policy. First, Ankara allowed for the safe transit of arms and fighters, many of whom were defectors from the Syrian Army, to various Syrian provinces. These defectors – who came to be known as the Free Syrian Army (FSA) – were given shelter by Turkey and were allowed to operate from a special refugee camp just inside its border with Syria (they would later be given permission to establish a presence in Turkish border towns).[22] Second, Ankara was eager to organise an opposition-in-exile and, controversially, sought to empower its favoured political party and ally, the Syrian Muslim

---

[19] Bassam Barabandi and Tyler Jess Thompson, 'A Friend of my Father: Iran's Manipulation of Bashar Al-Assad', Atlantic Council, 28 August 2014.
[20] *Ibid.*; Simon Tisdall, 'Iran and Turkey's Meeting Reveals New Approach to Syria', *Guardian*, 25 October 2012.
[21] Nada Bakri, 'Syria Reverses Ban on Imported Goods', *International Herald Tribune*, 6 October 2011.
[22] Liam Stack, 'In Slap at Syria, Turkey Shelters Anti-Assad Fighters', *New York Times*, 27 October 2011.

Brotherhood – a policy that eventually helped to fracture the budding rebel alliance. Third, with French and Arab support, Ankara, starting in November 2011, began to advocate for international intervention in Syria. Turkey supported the creation of a buffer zone along pockets of its border with Syria, which would be protected by a no-fly zone – the establishment of which would require the destruction of Syria's air defence and military installations.[23]

Ankara envisioned that the rebels would use this safe zone to establish a rival government to that of Assad's in Damascus.[24] In turn, this nascent government would secure support from local Syrians via its provision of services and then be recognised as the official Syrian government by the international community. (However, this proposal ultimately stalled due to the US's reluctance to intervene, and the inability of the backers of the Syrian rebels – Turkey included – to establish a credible and united opposition.)

At that time, Turkey assumed that Assad would fall within six months of sanctions being imposed in November. The result was that Ankara was eager to play a prominent role in the creation of a post-Assad Syrian state that would reflect the AKP's overarching interests in the Middle East. Ankara's thinking was further influenced by Turkey's popularity after the Arab upheavals (in a 2012 poll, 69 per cent of those surveyed across the Middle East had a favourable view of Turkey),[25] the subsequent empowerment of the Muslim Brotherhood in Tunisia and Egypt, and its belief that Turkey was on the cusp of creating a new regional order.[26] Having made the decision to sever ties with the Assad regime, therefore, the AKP perceived an opportunity to help deliver a political entity in Syria that would allow Ankara to further expand its influence within a changing Middle East.

To assist with this, Ankara allied with Qatar – a fellow supporter of the Muslim Brotherhood with a similar outlook on the future of Islamist politics in the Middle East. The two countries also backed the creation of the rebel group Liwa Al-Tawhid, which further benefited from the support of the Brotherhood in Aleppo.[27] The two countries eventually formed a

---

[23] Adrian Blomfield, 'France Calls for Tough Sanctions on Syria', *Daily Telegraph*, 18 November 2011.

[24] Christopher Philips, 'Into the Quagmire: Turkey's Frustrated Syria Policy', Chatham House, December 2012.

[25] Mensur Akgun and Sabiha Senyucel Gundogar, 'The Perception of Turkey in the Middle East 2012', Turkish Economic and Social Studies Foundation, 2012.

[26] Taha Ozhan, 'Egypt Turkey Axis and the New Middle East Geopolitics', Foundation for Political, Economic and Social Research, 17 November 2012.

[27] *Ibid.*; Aron Lund, 'The Politics of the Islamic Front, Part 1: Structure and Support', Carnegie Endowment for International Peace, 14 January 2014.

symbiotic relationship. Qatar helped to fund the groups Turkey supported, whilst Turkish non-governmental organisations (NGOs) hosted and facilitated meetings with early defectors, and then began sending both military and humanitarian aid to individual brigades operating in Syria.[28]

As an example of this, in May 2011, the Brotherhood had sent a delegation to the second meeting held in Turkey to organise a Syrian opposition. In parallel, the group had begun to organise the creation of rebel brigades in Homs, Hama, Idlib and Aleppo.[29] In September, with Ankara having formally changed its policy *vis-à-vis* Syria, Syrian opposition figures gathered in two hotels in Istanbul to finalise the list of representatives that would make up the official Syrian opposition. Thereafter, the Syrian Muslim Brotherhood emerged as the dominant member of the Syrian National Council (SNC), using its influence with Turkey to engender support from defecting Syrian Army officers. According to Hassan Hassan, an analyst at the Delma Institute in Abu Dhabi, 'The Brotherhood asked for their loyalty and, in return, the group promised to pressure Turkey to create a buffer zone along its border with Syria'.[30]

These efforts pre-date Ankara's formal endorsement of the buffer-zone proposal in November 2011, and demonstrate the extent to which the AKP and the Syrian Muslim Brotherhood were aligned in the early days of the conflict. The Brotherhood's influence extended to the leadership of the FSA. However, Turkey's support for the Brotherhood, combined with the group's over-representation in the SNC, helped to fracture the alliance of countries supportive of Syrian rebels.[31] These regional fault lines reflected those that had first appeared shortly after the overthrow of Mubarak in Egypt and President Zine El Abidine Ben Ali in Tunisia in 2011. The leadership in Saudi Arabia, the UAE, Jordan and

---

[28] The conservative Turkish NGO Imkander posted a series of YouTube videos of its aid workers providing food aid and tending to wounded Liwa Al-Tawhid fighters in a makeshift hospital in Gaziantep, Turkey. See Imkander, 'IMKANDER Suriyeli Yaralilarin Yaninda', YouTube, 10 March 2014.

[29] Hassan Hassan, 'How the Muslim Brotherhood Hijacked Syria's Revolution', *Foreign Policy*, 13 March 2013.

[30] *Ibid.*

[31] According to Charles Lister, 'Meanwhile, political groupings within the SNC and their foreign allies fostered relationships with specific armed opposition groups, reproducing the political factionalism of the SNC within the insurgency. This did little to shore up the SNC's reputation within Syria, however. Many ridiculed exiled SNC representatives for being more familiar with the comforts of five star hotels than the realities of war-torn Syria'. See Charles Lister, 'Dynamic Stalemate: Surveying Syria's Military Landscape', Brookings Doha Center, 19 May 2014.

Bahrain viewed the ascendance of the Muslim Brotherhood as a threat. Turkey and Qatar, on the other hand, saw it as an advantage, albeit for different reasons.[32] These differences in perceptions of the Brotherhood impacted regional support for the SNC after it was first formed in 2011 and resulted in the creation of the National Coalition for Syrian Revolutionary and Opposition Forces – more commonly referred to as the Syrian National Coalition (henceforth, the National Coalition) – in 2012.[33] The SNC was just one of the groups represented in the National Coalition, filling only twenty-two seats out of sixty.[34]

Throughout 2012, Qatar was able to retain its position as the most influential backer of the Syrian opposition. However, when elections were held for the position of chairman of the National Coalition in July 2013, Saudi Arabia's preferred candidate, Ahmad Al-Jarba, was re-elected despite Qatar's backing for Syria's former prime minister, Riad Hijab. In response, Hijab, another Qatari proxy, Mustafa Sabbagh, and forty-three other members withdrew from the National Coalition.[35] Sabbagh only re-joined the coalition in March 2014 after Saudi Arabia, the UAE and Bahrain had withdrawn their diplomatic personnel from Qatar.

These regional schisms led Turkey to adopt a schizophrenic policy in relation to the various Syrian rebel groups. On the one hand, Turkey worked diligently to support the National Coalition. To facilitate closer co-operation between Syria's political opposition and rebel groups on the ground, in December 2012 the West and many Arab states created a central organising body within the FSA, the Supreme Military Council (SMC), through which international backers could finance and arm certain rebel groups. However, due to infighting and different points of view about the numerous rebel groups, many of these international backers continued to arm individual brigades outside of this formal structure.[36] Turkey was no exception and has maintained its support for non-FSA related groups, even though this policy undermined the very coalition it was seeking to empower. The fact that these two policies were at odds with one another had a significant, negative

---

[32] Aaron Stein and Michael Stephens, 'Where Did it All Go Wrong? The Qatar-Turkey Power House Comes Up Short', RUSI.org, 14 January 2014.

[33] See Carnegie Endowment for International Peace, 'The National Coalition for Syrian Revolutionary and Opposition Forces', <http://carnegieendowment.org/syriaincrisis/?fa=50628>, accessed 9 November 2014.

[34] *Ibid.*

[35] Yezid Sayigh, 'The Syrian Opposition's Bleak Outlook', Carnegie Endowment for International Peace, 17 April 2014.

[36] International Crisis Group (ICG), 'Rigged Cars and Barrel Bombs: Aleppo and the State of the Syrian Civil War', Middle East Report No. 155, 9 September 2014.

impact on one of Turkey's main priorities: the unification of the Syrian opposition.

Turkey's favouring of three rebel groups in particular – Liwa Al-Tawhid, Ansar Al-Sham, Ahrar Al-Sham[37] – undermined the National Coalition's influence on rebel groups on the ground and highlights the paradoxical nature of Turkish policy in this period. For example, Ahrar's leadership had close links to Al-Qa'ida affiliate Jabhat Al-Nusra.[38] Moreover, according to the International Crisis Group, in September 2013, following the US's decision not to strike the Syrian regime in response to its chemical-weapons attack on Damascus in the previous month, the group joined with Al-Nusra, Liwa Al-Tawhid, Jaish Al-Islam and Saqour Al-Sham in denouncing the National Coalition. Two months later, Ahrar Al-Sham, Liwa Al-Tawhid, Jaish Al-Islam and Saqour Al-Sham announced their intention to form the Islamic Front, which, they stated, would not have any formal ties with the Western-supported SMC – the umbrella body created to arm the Syrian rebels.[39]

However, it appears that Turkey has since come under considerable pressure to revise its relationship with such groups – especially after the US began to take a more active role in the Syrian conflict, with its emphasis on empowering Saudi Arabia over Qatar. In turn, it appears that Turkey has put pressure on these groups to change their own affiliations. In May 2014, for example, the Islamic Front released a 'Revolutionary Covenant', which served as a 'common framework' of principles to which its component groups subscribed. The document did not include a reference to an Islamic State as being the ideal form of governance in a post-Assad Syria. Instead, according to Charles Lister of the Brookings Institution, 'If rumors are to be believed, the Islamic Front, and particularly Ahrar al-Sham, had recently been forced into a corner by its backer/s ... [to] "publicly distance yourself from Al-Qaeda (Jabhat al-Nusra) or lose your plentiful support"'.[40] Moreover, after coming under pressure from Qatar – and presumably Turkey – eighteen rebel factions, including Ahrar Al-Sham joined the Revolutionary Command Council in August

---

[37] Ahrar Al-Sham formed in the Idlib and Hama regions after Assad released Islamist political prisoners in early 2011. Interview with Charles Lister, a visiting fellow at the Brookings Doha Center, 25 October 2014.

[38] Aron Lund, 'Syria's Ahrar Al-Sham Leadership Wiped Out in Bombing', Carnegie Endowment for International Peace, 9 September 2014; *BBC News*, 'Leading Syrian Rebel Groups Form New Islamic Front', 22 November 2013.

[39] ICG, 'Rigged Cars and Barrel Bombs: Aleppo and the State of the Syrian Civil War'.

[40] Charles Lister, 'Reading Between the Lines: Syria's Shifting Dynamics or More of the Same?', *Huffington Post*, 29 May 2014.

2014.[41] As such, the group appeared to be publicly distancing itself from Al-Nusra.[42]

In June 2014, Turkey also joined with much of the international community in designating Al-Nusra a terrorist organisation. Ankara had hitherto resisted the US's favoured approach of blacklisting the group,[43] even though this placed it at odds with all of its Western allies, as well as most of the Gulf Arab states, for four reasons. First, there was a perception in Ankara that it could work closely with, and potentially moderate, hard-line rebel groups such as Al-Nusra in Syria. Second, Al-Nusra had worked closely with other Turkish-backed rebel groups, most notably Ahrar Al-Sham, as well as other groups operating under the FSA umbrella. Third, and linked to this, Turkey perceived Al-Nusra as a 'Syrian group' fighting against the regime for the future of all Syrians. Fourth, the rebels relied heavily on Al-Nusra to make gains against the regime. According to Lister, 'The unrivalled ability of Jabhat al-Nusra suicide operatives to break through established military defences makes it a force that the insurgency as a whole would struggle to live without, for now. After all, the recent gains in Idlib between 23–26 May [2014] were only made possible by at least six large suicide vehicle bombings, all by Jabhat al-Nusra fighters'.[44]

Crucial to this policy of supporting Al-Nusra was Turkey's relationship with Qatar, which in turn relied on a number of middlemen and financiers in the Gulf to finance its proxies in the Syrian conflict.[45] According to Elizabeth Dickinson, Middle East and Africa correspondent for *Christian Science Monitor* and *The National*, 'Throughout 2012 and early 2013, activist Salafists in Kuwait teamed up with Syrian expatriates to build, fund, and supply extremist brigades that would eventually become groups such as al-Nusra Front and its close ally, Ahrar al-Sham'.[46] This money was routed through middlemen based in Turkey, who operated with the tacit acceptance of Ankara.

---

[41] The Council operates outside of the National Coalition, but includes the US-supported rebel groups Syrian Revolutionaries Front and Harakat Hazm. *Daily Star* (Lebanon), 'Eighteen Rebel Factions Announce New Military Grouping', 4 August 2014.
[42] Lund, 'Syria's Ahrar Al-Sham Leadership Wiped Out in Bombing'.
[43] Abigail Fielding-Smith, 'US Labels Syrian Rebel Group "Terrorists"', *Financial Times*, 11 December 2012.
[44] Lister, 'Reading Between the Lines'.
[45] Elizabeth Dickinson, 'Playing with Fire: Why Private Gulf Financing for Syria's Rebels Risks Igniting Sectarian Conflicts at Home', Analysis Paper No. 16, Saban Center for Middle East Policy at Brookings, December 2013.
[46] Elizabeth Dickinson, 'The Case against Qatar', *Foreign Policy*, 30 September 2014.

Turkey was able to maintain support for this policy up until early 2014 but under increased US pressure it shifted its tactics – compelling Ahrar to distance itself from Al-Nusra and formally designating the latter as a terrorist organisation. This same period also saw the introduction of US-manufactured TOW anti-tank missiles into the conflict, which appear to have been supplied by Saudi Arabia through Jordan and Turkey to select rebel groups.[47] This suggests that in May or June 2014, the conflicting strategies of the US, Saudi Arabia, Qatar and Turkey *vis-à-vis* the Syrian conflict became more closely aligned, based on a commitment to strengthening certain rebel brigades in the battle against both the Assad regime and IS.[48]

Turkey's ongoing role in this current strategy is critical. The CIA, operating from a military operations command centre (MOC) in the Turkish border city of Reyhanli, is working closely with Turkey's MIT to slow funding to Islamist groups and instead channel the payment of salaries to, and provision of ammunition for, thousands of vetted rebels.[49] Liwa Al-Tawhid and Ahrar Al-Sham are not on the list of rebel groups to receive support via this command centre. Instead, aid is distributed to the US- and Saudi-backed Syrian Revolutionaries Front (SRF) and Harakat Hazm.[50] The decrease in aid to the Islamic Front has, however, degraded the group's effectiveness in areas like Aleppo and Idlib, a potential outcome previously emphasised by Turkey in justifying its support for the group.

Moreover, since support has been increased for certain rebel proxies, Al-Nusra began to clash with the now Turkish-supported SRF in northwestern Idlib, with the former taking control of the five border towns of Binnish, Harem, Sarmada, Darkoush and Salqin in July 2014, for example.[51] At that time, the group's military operations, according to Lister, pointed to 'an attempt to isolate rebels from the MOC supply line through the Bab al-Hawa crossing and potentially also to take advantage of this period of disunity within the Islamic Front'.[52] They may also have been an attempt to demonstrate that it no longer co-operated with other Syrian rebel groups in order to undercut the appeal of IS, whose

---

[47] Karen DeYoung, 'Syrian Opposition Fighters Obtain U.S.-Made TOW Antitank Missiles', *Washington Post*, 16 April 2014.
[48] Lister, 'Reading Between the Lines'.
[49] Ben Hubbard, 'U.S. Goal is to Make Syrian Rebels Viable', *New York Times*, 18 September 2014.
[50] Aron Lund, 'The Syrian Revolutionaries' Front', Carnegie Endowment for International Peace, 13 December 2013; Patrick J McDonnell, 'Lack of Reliable Partners in Syria Poses Daunting Challenge to U.S.', *Los Angeles Times*, 23 September 2014.
[51] Charles Lister, 'The "Real" Jabhat Al-Nusra Appears to Be Emerging', *Huffington Post*, 7 October 2014.
[52] *Ibid.*

emergence has threatened Al-Qa'ida Core's leadership and its position as the vanguard of international jihadism.[53]

More recently, Ankara has helped to create yet another umbrella group, known as the Syrian Revolutionary Command Council (RCC). The most dominant rebel group under this umbrella is Ahrar Al-Sham, together with some FSA brigades operating in the north. The RCC claims to have the support of seventy different rebel groups and all have pledged 100 fighters each to form a new 'Syrian National Army' to combat the regime and the Islamic State. The umbrella does not include Jabhat Al-Nusra, which is yet another indication of Ahrar's Turkish-backed efforts to distance itself from the group.[54]

Turkey's former policy of 'benign neglect' with regards to IS and its direct support of Al-Nusra in certain instances has backfired.[55] As the latter has come under threat from the growing appeal of IS, it is relying more heavily on tactics reminiscent of those previously used by Al-Qa'ida Core and its other affiliates. Moreover, Al-Nusra has overrun both the SRF and Harakat Hazam – the groups that the US and Turkey had hoped would be able to expand their influence in Syria – with both groups surrendering in early November 2014 in northern Idlib after months of clashes, for example.[56]

Ankara therefore now has to contend with two different jihadist groups that control large swathes of territory along its border, one of which it had previously supported.

The PKK Threat: Failure to Prevent Kurdish Enclaves in Syria

The outbreak of protests in Syria in March 2011 caused concern amongst Turkish officials about the breakdown of central government control over the country's Kurdish-majority provinces. This concern stems from Turkey's decades-old civil conflict with its own Kurdish group, the PKK. The AKP had begun peace negotiations with PKK leader Abdullah Ocalan in 2006, but the talks progressively broke down between 2009 and 2012. According to the International Crisis Group's unofficial, open-source count, at least 920 people have been killed during this period, of which

---

[53] Ben Hubbard, 'ISIS Threatens Al Qaeda as Flagship Movement of Extremists', *New York Times*, 30 June 2014.

[54] Marlin Dick, 'Syrian Rebel Coalition Announced', *Daily Star*, 1 December 2014. Tweets posted by Charles Lister on 1 December 2014 illustrate the group's command structure: <https://twitter.com/Charles_Lister/status/539350013646995456>, accessed 16 December 2014.

[55] Richard Spencer and Raf Sanchez, 'Turkish Government Co-operated with Al-Qaeda in Syria, Says Former US Ambassador', *Daily Telegraph*, 12 September 2014.

[56] Syrian Observatory for Human Rights, 'Jabhat Al-Nusra Clashes with the Syrian Revolutionaries Front in Idlib Countryside', 28 October 2014.

304 were members of Turkish security forces, 533 were PKK members and ninety-one were civilians.[57]

The AKP was forced to recalibrate its approach to the Kurdish issue in 2012, following a spike in casualties in Turkey as well as a series of rebel gains in Syria, which prompted Assad partially to withdraw his forces from the country's Kurdish regions in mid-July 2012.[58] The PYD seized the opportunity and took control of civic buildings in Jazira, Kobane and Afrin, towns now collectively known as Rojava. Taken aback by these territorial gains, Erdogan threatened to intervene, declaring: 'We will not let the terrorist group set up camps [in northern Syria] and pose a threat to us ... No one should attempt to provoke us. We will not bow to provocation but rather take whatever steps are necessary against terrorism'.[59] In reality, Turkey had no intention of intervening in Syria and this threat was intended only to coerce the PYD to accede to its demands; however, this failed.

In response to the PYD's consolidation of power in Rojava, Turkey pursued a short-sighted policy that simultaneously failed to prevent the group from establishing autonomy and undermined its closest Kurdish ally: Masoud Barzani, the president of the Kurdistan Regional Government (KRG) of northern Iraq and the leader of the Kurdistan Democratic Party (KDP). In 2011, Turkey first sought to curb the PYD's power in the cantons by supporting the Kurdish National Council (KNC) – an umbrella group of sixteen smaller Kurdish parties active in Syria. Some of these were allied to Barzani's KDP while others were affiliated with Jalal Talabani – the leader of Iraqi Kurdistan's Patriotic Union of Kurdistan (PUK).[60]

In July 2012, the PYD and the KNC agreed to the Erbil Declaration, under which they would govern Rojava jointly – an agreement that would be facilitated by the establishment of the Supreme Kurdish Committee, which was also set out by the Declaration. Ankara was initially caught off guard by this rapprochement and worried that the agreement paved the way for Kurdish autonomy in Syria. Erdogan, for example, accused the PYD of secretly colluding with the Assad regime to engineer the withdrawal of Syrian government forces from Kurdish areas.[61] Given that the Erbil Declaration was never implemented owing to the stark

---

[57] E-mail correspondence with Hugh Pope, Deputy Program Director at the International Crisis Group's Istanbul office, 13 October 2014.

[58] ICG, 'Turkey: The PKK and a Kurdish Settlement', Europe Report No. 219, 11 September 2012.

[59] *Today's Zaman*, 'Don't Provoke Us, Erdogan Says in Stern Warning to Syrian Kurds', 26 July 2012.

[60] ICG, 'Syria's Kurds: A Struggle within a Struggle', Middle East Report No. 136, 22 January 2013.

[61] *Ibid.*

disagreements about its power-sharing and security provisions,[62] Ankara's concerns in this regard appear to have been premature. However, Ankara subsequently sought to take advantage of this failure to further isolate the PYD and to empower the KNC. First, in contrast to its policy in the Arab-majority areas of Syria, the AKP kept its borders with the three cantons of Rojava closed – a decision it only reversed in September 2014 when it opened a border gate with Kobane. In this regard, Turkey found common cause with the KDP and Barzani, who, after the Erbil Declaration failed, had closed the main border crossing between Iraqi and Syrian Kurdistan. Second, Ankara opened up a channel for dialogue with the PYD in order to coerce the group to adhere to its demands regarding the group's relationship with the PKK and its future plans for autonomy.

However, Ankara's longstanding support for the Syrian Muslim Brotherhood inadvertently undermined these efforts. The KNC criticised the AKP for its support for 'Islamists', a Brotherhood-dominated government and a constitution that did not mention the Kurds. According to journalist Jake Hess, the KNC 'complained about the Syrian opposition's "intransigence and perceived domination by the Syrian Muslim Brotherhood (SMB) and Turkey"'.[63] Its meetings with the SNC, said Kurdish officials, were 'no different than they were with the Baathists'.[64] It is no surprise, therefore, that the PYD did not join the National Coalition and instead worked to solidify its control over the cantons of Afrin, Kobane and Jazira.

Ankara's support for Al-Nusra and the FSA in opposition to the PYD also served to undermine Ankara's relationship with the latter, while the former two proved too weak to unseat the PYD from the canton of Jazira (a situation which foreshadowed that of summer and autumn 2014, in relation to Kobane). The extent to which Turkey's strategy had backfired first became clear during the Battle of Ras Al-Ayn, which began in November 2012 when some 200 fighters from Al-Nusra and the PYD's militia, the People's Protection Units (YPG), clashed on the outskirts of the largest Kurdish canton in Syria, Jazira.[65] During the clashes, reports emerged that a number of Syrian opposition fighters had crossed the Turkey-Syria border to fight against the YPG in Ras Al-Ayn and the

---

[62] ICG, 'The Flight of Icarus? The PYD's Precarious Rise in Syria', Middle East Report No. 151, May 2014.
[63] Jake Hess, 'Washington's Secret Back-Channel Talks with Syria's Kurdish Terrorists', *Foreign Policy*, 7 October 2014.
[64] *Ibid.*
[65] *Al Arabiya News*, 'Jihadist Rebels in Standoff with Syria Kurds: NGO', 22 November 2012; *Al Jazeera*, 'Syria Rebels Clash with Armed Kurds', 19 November 2012.

neighbouring territory of Kobane.[66] Turkey denied the reports, but Erdogan nevertheless praised the advances made against the PYD.[67] A ceasefire agreed in late November failed to stop the fighting,[68] but in late January 2013, representatives of the Supreme Kurdish Committee met with Michael Kilo, a representative of the SNC, to broker a more comprehensive ceasefire agreement. The ceasefire that was agreed in February stipulated the establishment of joint FSA-YPG checkpoints; the creation of a local council comprising the SNC, PYD and KNC; the removal of foreign fighters from the area; and – perhaps most importantly – a pledge to work together to overthrow the regime.[69] Although Al-Nusra did not participate directly in the negotiations, it also agreed to abide by the provisions. The agreement appeared to suffer a serious setback when, three days after its signature, Salim Idris, then chief of staff of the FSA's Supreme Military Council, rejected the accord, citing the PYD's links to the PKK and the influx of Iranian Kurds to bolster the ranks of the YPG's units in Syria and Iraqi Kurdistan.[70] However, the clashes between the FSA and Al-Nusra and the PYD subsided, and the latter continued its efforts to create the conditions for autonomous governance in all three Kurdish cantons on the Syrian-Turkish border.

Nevertheless, Turkey's rhetorical, and perhaps direct, support for Al-Nusra had long-term consequences for its overarching efforts to isolate the PYD in Syria. After the sustained clashes with Al-Nusra, the Assad regime – perhaps as part of a larger effort to punish Turkey for its support of the Syrian rebels – began to supply weapons to the PYD. Moreover, from October 2013 the PYD was able to circumvent the Turkish and KDP closure of the border crossings, after its fighters seized control of the Yaroubiyeh border crossing that links Jazira with Iraqi territory controlled – until recently – by Baghdad; thus providing the canton with a critical source of supplies.[71]

In this way, Turkey's policies ultimately strengthened both the PYD in Syria and the PKK in Turkey, with which it had recently restarted peace

---

[66] ICG, 'Blurring the Borders: Syrian Spillover Risks for Turkey', Europe Report No. 225, 30 April 2013.

[67] Enis Berberoglu, 'Despite US Opposition, Oil Trade with Iraq is Legal, PM Erdogan Says', *Hurriyet Daily News*, 8 February 2013.

[68] *Agence France Presse*, 'Raging Clashes Pit Syrian Kurds against Jihadists', 18 January 2011; KurdWatch.org, 'Ra's Al-'Ayn: No Easing of Tensions Despite Agreement between PYD and Free Syrian Army', 4 January 2013.

[69] *Firatnews.com*, 'Agreement in Serekaniye', 18 February 2013.

[70] Fehim Tateskin, 'Syria: Difficult to Read New Kurdish-FSA Alliance', *Al-Monitor*, 22 February 2013.

[71] ICG, 'The Flight of Icarus?'.

negotiations.[72] Thus, when PYD leader Salih Muslim visited the director of MIT, Hakan Fidan, and representatives of the Foreign Ministry in Ankara in July 2013, the PYD's state-building efforts were reportedly on the agenda, with Fidan agreeing to the creation of an autonomous Kurdish area in Syria so long as the PYD joined the National Coalition and turned its attention to fighting Assad. Muslim, in turn, is reported to have promised Fidan that the PYD would not launch terror attacks in Turkey.[73]

This was a subtle change in policy on Turkey's part. On the one hand, Ankara was still conditioning the creation of a federal, post-Assad state on the acceptance of the concept by the National Coalition. However, on the other hand, Ankara – perhaps for the first time – signalled its willingness to accept a decentralised state that recognised the PYD as a legitimate political party. The two sides, however, remained at loggerheads over two issues: the PYD's hands-off approach in attempting to bring down the Syrian regime and its relationship with the PKK.

Kurdish Politics and the Rise of IS

In March 2013, some 2 million people gathered in Turkey's Kurdish-majority city of Diyarbakir to celebrate Newroz (the Kurdish new year). At the event, two members of parliament from the pro-Kurdish People's Democratic Party (HDP) read a letter by the PKK leader Adbullah Ocalan, written in similar language to that used by Ahmet Davutoglu. Ocalan wrote: 'For the past 200 years, conquest wars, western imperialists [sic] interventions and oppressive mentalities have urged Arabic, Turkish, Persian and Kurdish entities to form artificial states, borderlines, problems. The era of exploiting, oppressive ignoring mentalities is over'. He added: 'A door is opening from a process of armed resistance to a process of democratic politics. A new process emphasizing on political, social and economic aspect is starting, a new mentality on democratic rights, freedoms and equality is developing'.[74] The letter did not directly refer to a possible ceasefire with the AKP, but rather indicated an embrace of democratic politics and a renewed effort to work with the AKP to find a solution to the Kurdish issue.[75] According to Hatem Ete, an adviser to

---

[72] According to an anonymous Turkish official cited by the International Crisis Group, 'We made the PYD stronger by trying to undermine it.' *Ibid.*
[73] *Today's Zaman*, 'PYD's Muslim: Ankara Agreed to Conditional Autonomy', 28 July 2013.
[74] *Euronews*, 'Full Transcript of Abdullah Ocalan's Ceasefire Call', 22 March 2013.
[75] Cengiz Candar, 'Ocalan's Message is Much More than a Cease-Fire', *Al-Monitor*, 24 March 2013.

Davutoglu, Ocalan's letter signalled 'a significant change in the PKK's roadmap from armed struggle to political struggle'.[76]

The AKP's response to this letter should be seen against the backdrop of its failure to prevent the establishment of PYD-administered cantons in Syria and escalating violence within Turkey's own borders. To address both of these threats, Ankara pursued a three-pronged strategy. First, it renewed negotiations with Ocalan and agreed to a ceasefire. Second, it worked to empower Barzani, president of the KRG in Iraq. Third, it continued its efforts to arm and provide aid to the Syrian opposition. These policies were designed to hasten the end of the conflict in Syria, while also putting in place an alternative political model for Syrian and Turkish Kurds, ostensibly based on the perceived economic success of the KDP in Iraqi Kurdistan. The strategy was intended to weaken the PKK, while also creating a roadmap for eventual peace with Abdullah Ocalan. The conflict in Syria, however, undermined these efforts and Ankara's support for a slew of anti-Assad rebel groups severely complicated its handling of the Kurdish issue.

To support its policy of regime change, Turkey also opened its border to foreign fighters. Ankara argued that the influx of foreign fighters, weapons and funding for certain rebel groups would help to hasten Assad's overthrow. It continued to pursue this policy until March 2014, after which it took steps to stem the flow of foreign fighters moving across its territory. Up until this point in the conflict, however, Turkey did little to prevent individuals from crossing the border with Syria, except in the areas controlled by the PYD, where border crossings remain closed.

This provides another instance in which a particular Turkish policy detracted from its broad objective of regime change in Syria. Ankara's border policy indirectly undermined the cohesion of the Syrian opposition and helped to empower Al-Nusra's one-time affiliate, IS.[77] The ties between the two groups were severed after Al-Nusra's leader, Abu Mohammad Al-Jolani, rejected the plan announced by IS leader Abu Bakr Al-Baghdadi to incorporate Al-Nusra into IS, and publicly affirmed his group's allegiance to Al-Qa'ida leader Ayman Al-Zawahiri.[78] However, while Al-Nusra continued to co-operate with members of the Turkish-backed Islamic Front and FSA thereafter, IS often resorted to vicious tactics that eventually, from January 2014, led to clashes with the Islamic Front. IS soon took control of Raqqa, which became its stronghold, as well as two

---

[76] Hatem Ete, 'What Ocalan's Newroz Letter Means for the Peace Process', *Daily Sabah*, 24 March 2014.

[77] ICG, 'Rigged Cars and Barrel Bombs'.

[78] *Ibid.* Turkey officially designated ISIS/Islamic State a terrorist organisation in October 2013, but did not include Al-Nusra in the list of such organisations until June 2014.

border crossings near the Syrian cities of Jarabulus and Tel Abyad that enabled it to control and protect the supply line to Raqqa. Moreover, an IS offensive initiated in August 2014 to the north and east of Aleppo threatened the border town of Azaz,[79] forcing Turkey to intermittently close the Oncupinar/Bab Al-Salameh crossing and thus to rely heavily on the Cilvegozu/Bab Al-Hawa border crossing, near the city of Reyhanli, to supply its preferred rebel proxies.[80]

Thus by late 2013, the advances made by IS in northern Syria, in combination with its clashes with other Turkish-backed rebel groups, threatened Ankara's goal of empowering its proxies to topple Assad. The group's increasing presence to the north of Aleppo, for example, disrupted Turkey's supply lines to its preferred rebel groups, Ahrar Al-Sham and Liwa Al-Tawhid. Moreover, the Syrian regime was able to use IS's rapid rise to further fragment the rebels' approach and, from November 2013, used IS's advances to the north of Aleppo to aid in its own military campaign to retake the city from the south.[81]

Moreover, the extent – and the complicated nature – of the links between numerous Syrian rebel groups and Al-Nusra has lessened the likelihood that the US will abandon its cautious approach to the conflict and fully embrace that pursued by Ankara instead. Absent robust US intervention, Ankara cannot fully achieve its primary aim of regime change in Syria; it does not have the military capability that would allow it to independently establish a no-fly zone or a buffer zone along its border with Syria, for example.[82] Moreover, if Turkey were to commit ground troops the resulting casualties would damage the AKP politically and detract from efforts to prepare for elections in June 2015. This has made Ankara's Syria policy contingent upon decisions made in Washington.

However, the AKP has thus far failed in its efforts to galvanise support from the Obama administration for its preferred policy. This ongoing disagreement has so far only grown more acute, not least because Turkey has only allowed the US to use the drones permanently stationed at Incirlik Air Base for surveillance missions along the Turkish-Syrian border. It continues to refuse to allow the US to use Turkish air bases for bombing missions targeting IS inside Syria and Iraq.

---

[79] *Ibid.*

[80] Fehim Tastekin, 'Turkey's Syria Borders an Open Door for Smugglers', *Al-Monitor*, 30 April 2014.

[81] Charles Lister, 'As ISIS Closes in, is it Game Over for Syria's Opposition in Aleppo?', *CNN*, 15 August 2014.

[82] Interview with Can Kasapoglu, a research fellow at the Istanbul-based Center for Economics and Foreign Policy Studies, 17 October 2014.

Turkey's Hostage Crisis

In March 2014, Turkey first began to take steps to better control its border and to crack down on the illegal sale of the oil pumped from oil fields in Syria by IS.[83] In parallel, Ankara began to work more closely with European intelligence agencies to try to stem the flow of foreign fighters transiting Turkish territory in order to enter Syria. At the time of writing, Ankara continues to complain that EU member states are not sharing enough information with it about the number and names of citizens leaving the EU for Syria, but reports indicate that the number of arrests being made at Turkish airports and along the Turkish-Syrian border have increased in recent months.[84]

Despite these moves, Turkey was caught off guard by the rapid advance made by IS in Iraq in the summer of 2014. Ankara had been warned about the impending IS capture of the Iraqi city of Mosul, but did not take any steps to evacuate diplomatic personnel from its consulate there.[85] Having overrun the city on 10 June, the militant group took forty-six Turkish hostages (along with three Iraqi staffers), including the consul general, Ozturk Yilmaz. In the days following the collapse of Mosul, IS forces advanced on Baghdad, eventually taking control of large swathes of territory extending from the outskirts of Aleppo in Syria to Tikrit in Iraq. In the Kurdistan region of Iraq, meanwhile, IS began pushing north and east from Mosul in a campaign that included a concerted effort to ethnically cleanse the heterogeneous region of Sinjar – home to a large population of Iraqi Christians and the Yazidis, whose ancient religion is scorned by IS. These populations, which lived on the outskirts of territory controlled by the Kurdistan Regional Government and which were allied with Masoud Barzani's KDP, were assigned protection by Barzani-aligned Peshmerga fighters. However, as IS fighters approached, the Peshmerga fled, prompting thousands of civilians also to flee to the relative safety of the Sinjar Mountains.[86]

It was the collapse of the Peshmerga, and the resultant threat to the KRG's capital, Erbil, that prompted the US, supported by other members of the international community, to commence an air campaign against IS

---

[83] Fehim Tateskin, 'Kacak hatlarla ID Petrol', *Al-Monitor*, 15 September 2014; Daniel Dombey, 'Turkey's Clampdown on Isis Bearing Fruit in Border Areas', *Financial Times*, 3 September 2014.

[84] Sinan Ulgen and F Doruk Ergun, 'A Turkish Perspective on the Rise of the Islamic Caliphate', Center for Economics and Foreign Policy Studies, EDAM Discussion Paper Series 2014/6, 1 September 2014.

[85] Amberin Zaman, 'Turkey Ignored Direct Warnings of ISIS Attack on Mosul', *Al-Monitor*, 12 June 2014; Asli Aydintasbas, 'ISID'le tum dunya icin savasiyoruz', *Milliyet*, 8 September 2014.

[86] Tim Lister, 'Dehydration or Massacre: Thousands Caught in ISIS Chokehold', *CNN*, 12 August 2014.

positions in Iraqi Kurdistan in August 2014. In parallel, the PKK, which has a strong presence in the northern Iraqi city of Makhmour, attacked IS positions near the Sinjar Mountains.[87] These efforts included a push east from Jazira by the YPG of Syrian Kurdistan. Together – and backed by US air strikes – these two groups were able to carve out a corridor through which Yazidi refugees could flee to Rojava.[88] In mid-August, US air forces working closely with Iraqi Peshmerga were able to dislodge IS from territory it had conquered near the Mosul Dam.[89]

The collapse of the Peshmerga, combined with that of the Iraqi security forces in Mosul, was a further setback for both Turkey's Syria policy and its regional ambitions. First, the PKK and YPG were able to gain territory in Sinjar that had hitherto been under the control of the Turkish-allied KDP. In turn, the YPG began to train Yazidi men in Jazira before sending them back to Sinjar in small units sympathetic to the PKK.[90] The PKK's carving out of territory in northern Iraq has since been met with suspicion by the KDP and concerns have been raised about any future effort to connect Sinjar to Jazira, on the Turkish-Syrian-Iraqi border. In parallel, the PYD and PKK have since won praise from Kurds for their role in the Yazidi crisis, whereas the KDP-allied Peshmerga's poor performance has been criticised. As a result, the PYD and PKK are now considered to be the most effective of the forces fighting against IS, which has therefore increased their appeal more broadly amongst Kurds, perhaps even at the expense of the KRG president, Masoud Barzani.

Turkey suffered its second setback in September 2014 when the KDP criticised its handling of the crisis. Commenting on Turkey's (lack of) assistance during the siege of Erbil, Fuad Hussein, the chief of staff to the president of the Kurdistan Regional Government, complained that 'They [Turkey] did not say they would not help. They said they would do so after Turkey's presidential election [in August] ... Every single Kurd is upset with Turkey's position. How would President Barzani not be upset about it? We are upset, because they did not help us when we needed them'.[91]

---

[87] Wladimir Van Wilgenburg, 'Kurdish Rivals Unite to Fight Islamic State', *Al Jazeera*, 16 August 2014.

[88] Joe Parkinson, 'Iraq Crisis: Kurds Push to Take Mosul Dam as U.S. Gains Controversial Guerrilla Ally', *Wall Street Journal*, 18 August 2014; Mutlu Civiroglu, 'How Kurdish Militias Have Successfully Fought Off the Islamic State', *Vice News*, 14 August 2014; Aris Roussinos, '"Everywhere Around is the Islamic State": On the Road in Iraq with YPG Fighters', *Vice News*, 14 August 2014.

[89] Helene Cooper, Mark Landler and Azam Ahmed, 'Troops in Iraq Rout Sunni Militants from a Key Dam', *New York Times*, 18 August 2014.

[90] Pomegranate Blog, 'Yazidis: Getting Ready to Fight Back', *The Economist*, 1 September 2014.

[91] Hevidar Ahmed, 'Senior Kurdistan Official: IS Was at Erbil's Gates; Turkey Did Not Help', Rudaw.net, 16 September 2014.

Ankara has prioritised its relationship with the KDP for many years, relying on Barzani and the KDP to act as a political counterweight to the PKK.[92] Yet, the rollback of the IS advance in Iraqi Kurdistan revealed not only a change in the balance of power in favour of the PKK and PYD, but also a frostier relationship with the KDP.

Indeed, these differences between Ankara and the KDP have only been exacerbated by the former's hesitation to join with US and allied air forces in bombing IS targets in both Syria and Iraq, and in their efforts to relieve the siege of Kobane. As will be discussed, the PYD's defence of the city has increased its broader appeal amongst Kurds and the international community. The ensuing media coverage of the clashes in Kobane has ended Turkey's de facto isolation of the PYD-controlled canton. Not only has Ankara now agreed to the further empowerment of the Syrian Kurds in fighting against Assad's forces, something that it had hitherto worked to impede;[93] but it has also now been forced to hasten ongoing discussions about sending a small contingent of KDP-allied Peshmerga to bolster the PYD in Kobane.[94] Furthermore, substantial disagreements over the air campaign against IS have continued to cause Turkey problems in its relationships with the US, the EU and the Gulf States, which in turn have been exacerbated by the Obama administration's refusal to pursue a policy of regime change in Syria.

Another thorny issue in Turkish–US relations is the AKP's apparent belief that the US used sectarianism as a tactic to keep the Iraqi state weak both before and after the 2003 invasion[95] – an approach that was continued thereafter by Iraq's former premier, Nouri Al-Maliki. As a solution to the issue of Iraqi sectarianism, Ibrahim Kalin, chief policy adviser to the Turkish president, has advocated that the country embrace *Tawhid* (oneness with, or acceptance of, Allah) as a source of political legitimacy. This proposal reflects the arguments put forward by Davutoglu – now Turkey's prime minister – and his promotion of *Tawhid* and *Tanzih* (a belief in the purity of Allah) as the political means by which to address sectarian grievances. This approach has since translated into Turkish support for the US-backed ousting of Al-Maliki and for the accession of

[92] Philip Robins, *Suits and Uniforms: Turkish Foreign Policy since the End of the Cold War* (Seattle, WA: University of Washington Press, 2003), pp. 318–42.
[93] Wladimir Van Wilgenburg and Vager Saadullah, 'Syrian Kurdish Factions Unite over Islamic State Threat', *Middle East Eye*, 24 October 2014.
[94] Ahmed Hussein, 'Nechirvan Barzani, Turkish PM Discuss ISIL's Threats on Region', *Iraqi News*, 30 September 2014; *Al Jazeera*, 'Iraqi Peshmerga Fighters Cross into Kobane', 1 November 2014.
[95] Ibrahim Kalin, 'To Keep Middle East Together, Don't Let Iraq Split Up', *Daily Sabah*, 20 June 2014; Tara Ozhan, 'New Borders No Panacea for Iraq Crisis', *Middle East Eye*, 9 July 2014; Tara Ozhan, 'Turkey's Iraq Challenge', *Hurriyet Daily News*, 13 June 2014.

Iraq's new prime minister, Haider Al-Abadi, in August 2014. In September 2014, President Erdogan called his Iraqi counterpart, Fuad Masum – who had assumed office only two months earlier – to congratulate him on the election of Abadi and to express a renewed interest in strengthening bilateral ties.[96] Davutoglu has since visited Abadi in Baghdad, where the two agreed to hold a joint cabinet meeting in December.[97]

Ankara has also expressed support for the undoing of Iraq's de-Ba'athification laws. Kalin argues that the law was a 'colossal mistake whereby not only the Sunni members of the Saddam era Iraq were isolated and penalized but also and more importantly the basic structures of the Iraqi state were destroyed'.[98] Similar arguments have been made by two other Turkish allies within the Iraqi political elite: Osama Al-Nujaifi, currently the vice president of Iraq, and his brother Atheel Al-Nujaifi, former governor of Nineveh Province. Osama has called for Sunni grievances to be addressed through the creation of a Sunni region[99] – a proposal on which Atheel expanded in an editorial for the *New York Times*, arguing for 'greater decentralization', before calling on 'Parliament [to] reverse Mr. Maliki's politicization of the security forces and establish new local forces to safeguard the population in Sunni areas, modeled after the Kurdish pesh merga. Only Sunni forces, with local support, can defeat ISIS in the areas it has seized'.[100]

Turkey has never explicitly supported this policy of greater Iraqi federalism, but its policies towards the KRG, combined with its support for the easing of de-Ba'athification, suggest that the AKP is at least supportive of the concept. Ankara is eager for Iraq to find a middle ground for the Sunni population, whereby structures are created to lure them away from both former Ba'athists and IS. However, as explored in Chapter II, Ankara's troubles with Baghdad – which began in 2009 after the AKP helped to create the Iraqiya political bloc in order to challenge Nouri Al-Maliki's Dawa Party – have prevented Turkey from playing an active role in Iraq following IS's takeover of Mosul. The primary interlocutors with Maliki, and thus key players in his standing down, were the US and

---

[96] *Hurriyet Daily News*, 'Turkish President Calls for Accelerated Ties with Iraqi Counterpart', 10 September 2014.
[97] *Daily Sabah*, 'Iraq PM: Turkey, Iraq Announce Key Agreement for Intelligence Sharing', 22 November 2014.
[98] Kalin, 'To Keep the Middle East Together, Don't Let Iraq Split Up'.
[99] 'Kurdistan's Exiled Nineveh Governor Calls to Form a Sunni Region: We No Longer Trust Iraqi Army', Ekurd.net, 2 July 2014, <http://www.ekurd.net/mismas/articles/misc2014/7/govt2316.htm>, accessed 4 November 2014.
[100] Rafe al-Esawi and Atheel al Nujaifi, 'Let Sunnis Defeat Iraq's Militants', *New York Times*, 27 July 2014.

Iran.[101] Turkey, in contrast, continues to work closely with Iraq's Sunni groups, many of which remain beset by infighting and have been weakened since the break-up of the Iraqiya coalition in 2012.

The net result is that Ankara now has established ties with Iraq's Sunni groups, but its relationship with Abadi remains tenuous.[102] As such, Turkey's preferred policies in Iraq have little chance of ever coming to fruition. Any attempt to reverse the de-Ba'athifcation laws, for example, is certain to fail due to continued Shia opposition to the idea. Indeed, having disavowed its ties with Iraq's Shia political parties in 2009, in favour of actively supporting the creation of a Sunni opposition, the AKP's influence is unsurprisingly limited. Moreover, as discussed in Chapter II, Osama Al-Nujaifi's Mutahidun Party – which is the party that Turkey has chosen to support since the collapse of the Iraqiya bloc – only controls twenty-seven seats in the Iraqi parliament (down from forty-five before the 2014 election). Ankara, in turn, has very little leverage with Iraqi politicians and its preferred policy proposals are thus unlikely to gain much traction inside Iraq. The reverberation of this political failure – largely precipitated by the decision taken five years ago to favour one religious group over another – is still being felt, having resulted in Turkish isolation.

The IS Coalition: Turkey Prioritises Syrian Regime Change

In September 2014, the forty-six hostages held by IS in Mosul since June were released.[103] Throughout the summer, Ankara had resisted overtures to join the coalition attacking IS,[104] arguing that the hostage situation 'tied its hands' and prevented it from participating in the air campaign.[105] However, Ankara's hesitancy was only partially based on concerns over the safety of the Turkish hostages.

Indeed, Ankara's reluctance betrays a different understanding of, and approach to, the threat posed by IS. It argues that the group is merely a symptom of Assad's brutal tactics; thus, in order to develop a comprehensive strategy to defeat IS, the coalition must first prioritise the

---

[101] Tim Arango, 'Maliki Agrees to Relinquish Power in Iraq', *New York Times*, 14 August 2014.

[102] Saban Kardas, 'Is Turkey's Long Game in Iraq a Success?', *Al Jazeera*, 3 September 2014.

[103] Emma Graham-Harrison, 'Turkey Celebrates Return of Hostages and Opens Border to Kurds Fleeing Isis', *Guardian*, 20 September 2014.

[104] Martin Chulov, Spencer Ackerman and Paul Lewis, 'US Confirms 14 Air Strikes against Isis in Syria', *Guardian*, 23 September 2014.

[105] Ilnur Cevik, 'Turkey Has a Vested Interest in Finishing Off ISIS, However...', *Daily Sabah*, 13 September 2014.

ousting of Assad.[106] The Obama administration, by contrast, has two aims: first, to degrade the group's military capacity, so as to prevent it from taking more ground, thereby threatening Iraqi territorial integrity; and second, to disrupt the group's operations, so that its members cannot easily plot and execute attacks against Western and Arab interests. These two goals are narrowly defined and incongruent with Turkey's emphasis on the Assad regime.[107]

Furthermore, the threat posed by IS has forced other Arab allies to publicly acknowledge a similar point of view to that of the US. The UAE, for example, views the threat posed by IS as being far more acute than that posed by the Assad regime. As such, the UAE has prioritised efforts to target the group, at the expense of its focus on regime change.[108] By contrast, the Saudis' perspective is similar to that of Turkey, albeit with the notable exception that Riyadh has opted to participate in the air campaign.[109] Qatar, Turkey's closest regional ally, has also recalibrated its regional strategy, having come under sustained criticism from other Gulf States for its support of the Muslim Brotherhood in recent years. Qatar has not directly participated in the US-led air strikes but it does support them, acquiescing in the use of the US Al-Udeid Air Base as a hub for the ongoing air campaign.[110] Finally, looking beyond state actors, both the PYD and the KDP have spoken in favour of the air strikes[111] – an unsurprising turn of events, given that the PYD has relied on a combination of US and Arab air power to stem an IS offensive in the Kurdish canton of Kobane, while the KDP has needed US air power to prevent the overrunning of Erbil.

The fact that Ankara has thus far conditioned its support for air strikes on the coalition prioritising regime change and the imposition of a number of 'safe zones' along the Turkish-Syrian border has therefore placed it in opposition to other coalition members.[112] Although it shares a mutual loathing for Assad with other allies, its absence from the coalition

---

[106] Ufuk Ulutas, 'The Coalition Needs to Do More against Assad', *New York Times*, 14 October 2014; Ibrahim Kalin, 'ISIS and the Assad Regime', *Daily Sabah*, 14 October 2014.

[107] Mina Al-Oraibi, 'Exclusive: General Allen Discusses Coalition Plans for Defeating ISIS as Regional Tour Starts', *Asharq Al-Awsat*, 25 October 2014.

[108] Ian Black, 'UAE's Leading Role against Isis Reveals its Wider Ambitions', *Guardian*, 30 October 2014.

[109] *CBS This Morning*, 'Saudi Prince on Helping US Fight ISIS', 25 September 2014.

[110] Mohamed Elshinnawi, 'Qatar Plays Delicate Role in Coalition Against IS Group', Voice of America, 15 October 2014.

[111] Yerevan Saeed, 'Kurdish Leader Calls for US Airstrikes around Kobane', Rudaw.net, 27 September 2014; Scott Peley, 'Iraq's Kurds Praise U.S. Support, Want More against ISIS', *CBS News*, 9 September 2014.

[112] *Al Jazeera Turk*, 'Turkiye'nin istedigi guvenli bolge', 16 October 2014, <http://www.aljazeera.com.tr/haber/turkiyenin-istedigi-guvenli-bolge>, accessed 4 November 2014.

reflects the incongruence of its policies with the more narrow aims of the US and other partners. This, in turn, has further isolated the AKP internationally while domestically, anger among Turkey's Kurds continues to rise, particularly over Ankara's handling of the IS assault on Kobane, which began in early July.[113] At the outset of the IS offensive against the weakest of the three Kurdish cantons, Turkey remained focused on the groups operating in Idlib and Aleppo, as well as the unfolding crisis in Iraq. To this end, Ankara did little to strengthen border patrols in areas around Kobane before the clashes between IS and the PYD prompted it to close the border to Turkish Kurds eager to join the PYD in defending the besieged city.[114] Instead, and as will be discussed below, Ankara agreed to allow Peshmerga allied with the KDP to transit its territory and enter Kobane to assist the PYD, alongside giving permission for the US to use its drones based at Incirlik Air Base for surveillance.[115]

The assault on Kobane, combined with the Al-Nusra assault on Ras Al-Ayn in 2012 against the Kurds, has engendered extreme Kurdish hostility towards the AKP.[116] This hostility has been augmented by growing sympathy for the plight of Kobane amongst a large number of Turkish Kurds, against what is perceived as an AKP-backed IS. The ranks of the YPG have been bolstered by Turkish Kurds, while PKK fighters from Tunceli have travelled to Kobane to assist in its defence,[117] with the result that a large number of Kurds from Turkey have been killed during the fighting, including the sons and daughters of elected Kurdish officials from municipalities in the Kurdish-majority southeast.[118] The funerals of some of these fighters, whose bodies have been returned home to Turkey, have been well attended, with Kurdish politicians frequently in

---

[113] Michael Stephens and Sofia Barbarani, 'While Iraq Burns, Isis Takes Advantage in Syria', *BBC News*, 18 July 2014.

[114] Author interview with Isabel Hunter, a Gaziantep-based independent journalist, 22 August 2014; Turkey Wonk, 'Turkey Turns a Blind Eye to the PKK', podcast, 22 August 2014.

[115] Rajiv Chandrasekaran, 'Syrians to be Trained to Defend Territory, Not Take Ground from Jihadists, Officials Say', *Washington Post*, 22 October 2014.

[116] Lauren Bohn, 'The Freedom Fight Has Returned to Turkey', *Foreign Policy*, 14 October 2014.

[117] Iason Athanasiadis, 'Is Turkey Sleepwalking into Trouble?', *Al Jazeera*, 8 August 2014.

[118] *Bugun*, 'BDP'li baskanin kizi Helin Demirkol Suriye'de olduruldu', 6 May 2014, <http://gundem.bugun.com.tr/suriyede-olduruldu-haberi/1092565>, accessed 4 November 2014; *Bestanuce*, 'BDP'li baskan Demirkol'un kizi Rojava'da hayatini kaybetti', 7 May 2014, <http://www.bestanuce1.com/haber/102527/bdp-li-baskan-demirkol-un-kizi-rojava-da-hayatini-kaybetti#sthash.AP9JBxnG.dpuf>, accessed 4 November 2014.

attendance.[119] Furthermore, concern for the citizens of Kobane has led to angry protests by Turkey's Kurdish population. Sustained clashes between Kurds sympathetic to the PYD and a minority of Islamist Kurds, affiliated with the political party Huda Par, have resulted in some forty deaths.[120] These clashes have since moved beyond Kurd-on-Kurd violence. At the time of writing, militants believed to have links to the PKK have shot and killed four members of the Turkish military in different cities and towns in the southeast of the country.[121] This low-level violence is not unprecedented, but it threatens to derail the fragile AKP-led peace process with PKK leader Abdullah Ocalan and to further complicate the AKP's Kurdish policies.

Turkey's response has only exacerbated the situation. Having left the border largely undefended for much of the summer, Ankara deployed tanks to the Mursitpinar border crossing to prevent both Turkish Kurds from crossing into Syria and YPG fighters from entering Turkey.[122] The images of Turkish tanks sitting idle on the border, while coalition aircraft bombed IS positions and YPG fighters battled IS in street-to-street battles, further undermined the AKP's global image, prompting more accusations from Kurdish and opposition politicians that the party in fact supports IS.[123]

In September, Turkey began to re-evaluate its PYD policy – which coincided with a similar reassessment on the part of the KDP, the ruling party of the Iraqi Kurdistan Regional Government, whose own hands-off approach to the Syrian Kurdish issue had likewise caused anger among its population. To this end, Prime Minister Ahmet Davutoglu met with his counterpart from the KRG, Nechirvan Barzani, in Ankara to discuss the possibility of Peshmerga fighters passing through Turkish territory before crossing the border into Syria, in order to bolster the Syrian Kurds fighting

---

[119] *DIHA*, 'Kobane'de yaşamini yitiren 4 YPG'linin cenazesi Suruç'a getirildi', 31 July 2014, <http://www.diclenews.com/tr/news/content/view/413023?page=17&from=2247095262>, accessed 4 November 2014; *DIHA*, 'YPG'li Polat'in cenazesi topraga verildi', 1 August 2014, <http://diclenews.com/tr/news/content/view/413160?page=10&from=3996974715>, accessed 4 November 2014.

[120] *Gazeteport*, 'Vali: PKK-HUDA PAR Catisiyor', 9 October 2014, <http://www.gazeteport.com.tr/haber/183013/vali-pkk-huda-par-catisiyor>, accessed 4 November 2014.

[121] *Hurriyet Daily News*, 'Another Turkish Soldier Killed, as Army Blames PKK', 29 October 2014.

[122] Jonny Hogg, 'Turkish Tanks Reinforce Border as ISIS Shells Kobani', *Reuters*, 29 September 2014; *Al Jazeera Turk*, 'Musul duserken neredeydiler?', 15 October 2014, <http://www.aljazeera.com.tr/haber/guvenli-bolgenin-sinirlarini-acikladi-0>, accessed 4 November 2014; *Anadolu Agency*, 'Turkish PM Calls for "All Inclusive" Syria Strategy', 16 October 2014.

[123] Seyfettin Kocak, 'Kilicdaroglu: AKP, ISID'e net ve acik bir destek veriyor', *Zaman*, 9 October 2014.

in Kobane.[124] The negotiations, by all accounts, proceeded slowly before the US decision to bypass Turkey and drop weapons and medical supplies from the air to the PYD on 20 October,[125] alongside an upturn in the number of coalition air strikes around the city.

The air drop embarrassed Turkish President Erdogan, who had indicated just hours earlier that Turkey would not allow the PYD to be armed because of its concerns about its connection to the PKK.[126] It also appears to have forced Ankara to hasten its discussion with the KDP about the sending of Peshmerga to Kobane, with Turkey announcing its support for this the following day – albeit under highly circumscribed conditions, including the careful auditing of the weapons sent to the city to ensure that they did not fall into the hands of the PYD's forces.[127] This rapid turn of events has further complicated Ankara's Syria policy. The surge in the appeal of the PYD has forced Turkey's ally the KDP to soften its stance on the group and – despite ongoing tensions – there are indications that Barzani has been forced to be more accepting of the PYD's ultimate aspirations for autonomy. Meanwhile, the PYD is continuing with its plans to hold elections in Rojava, which it is all but certain to win. Thus, after nearly three years of working to prevent Kurdish autonomy, Ankara is now faced with what appears to be a political *fait accompli* and thus the necessity of accepting some semblance of PYD-led Kurdish autonomy in Syria.

A Region in Crisis, an Isolated Ankara

The chaos in Syria has seriously undermined Ankara's foreign-policy ambitions in the Middle East. The AKP originally sought to leverage its close relationship with Bashar Al-Assad to anchor Aleppo to Anatolia, and thereby reconnect the city to its Ottoman hinterland; in turn, it was supposed, the area would benefit economically and, aided by a liberalised visa regime, could help to hasten the creation of a region with blurred borders.

Ankara did not officially sever ties with the Assad regime until November 2011, at which point Turkey believed that the regime's days were numbered and therefore set about installing its preferred proxies in the Syrian opposition. The AKP's belief in the fragility of the regime

---

[124] Ahmed Hussein, 'Nechirvan Barzani, Turkish PM Discuss ISIL's Threats on Region', *Iraqi News*, 30 September 2014.

[125] Fulya Ozerkan and Sara Hussein, 'US Air Drops, Turkey Boost Kurd Battle against Jihadists', *Agence France Presse*, 20 October 2014.

[126] *Today's Zaman*, 'Erdogan Opposes Arming PYD, Says it's a Terrorist Group Like PKK', 19 October 2014.

[127] Ugur Ergan, 'Turkish Intelligence Coordinates Peshmerga Crossing to Syria', *Hurriyet Daily News*, 28 October 2014.

proved incorrect, however. Thus, as the conflict continued, its decisions to back the Syrian Muslim Brotherhood and to open its border to foreign fighters helped to further fracture the anti-Assad coalition it was hoping to build.

Despite these challenges, the AKP has stuck to its preferred policy of regime change over all else. Ankara continues to argue that IS is a symptom of Assad's brutality. Thus, in order to defeat the group, one must attack the root cause: the regime. Ankara's arguments have so far failed to convince the US, whose mission remains focused on the stability of Iraq, the standing-up of the Iraqi Army, the training of a new rebel force in Syria and the degradation of IS. Turkey does have a role to play in this effort; it has offered to train a rebel force for the fight against both the Assad regime and IS in Syria, and has taken measures to crack down on the transit of men and materiél through its borders.

In sum, the evolution of the conflict in Syria has left Ankara flummoxed. The AKP has been unable to sway the US to adopt its preferred policy approach or goals and all of its efforts to suppress Kurdish autonomy have thus far failed. This has resulted in the AKP hardening its policy positions and refusing to join many of its allies in attacking IS. More broadly, the net result of the ongoing conflicts in Iraq and Syria has been to undermine Ankara's regional ambitions. Since the ousting of President Mohamed Morsi in Egypt in July 2013, the trajectory of Middle Eastern politics has placed Ankara at odds with much of the region. Moreover, the position of many of its regional allies – including Sunni Arab politicians in Iraq, its proxies in the Syrian political opposition, Masoud Barzani of the KRG, and the Muslim Brotherhood more generally – has been weakened in recent months. Across the region, Ankara is on the defensive and – beyond Qatar, Gaza and Erbil – has failed to maintain the carefully cultivated partnerships that it had pursued before the start of the Arab upheavals. This, in combination with persistent tensions with its Western allies, has left Turkey's government isolated and with little influence at a time when many of the region's current conflicts touch directly upon its core interests.

Nevertheless, the AKP remains assured that, in playing the 'long game' in the region, its foreign-policy decisions will ultimately be vindicated. As the next chapter will discuss, this means that the AKP continues to have faith in the viability of its foreign policy, with the result that no major changes should be expected in the foreseeable future.

V. 'PRECIOUS LONELINESS'

In September 2011, a confident Prime Minister Erdogan visited Libya, Tunisia and Egypt to express Ankara's support for democratic change in the Middle East. After nearly a decade of implementing its foreign policy of strategic depth, the Justice and Development Party (AKP) felt that the Arab upheavals had provided Ankara with the opportunity to create a new regional order that placed Turkey at the centre of a region governed by Muslim Brotherhood-affiliated parties. Having previously prioritised relationships with regional autocrats, September 2011 thus saw the AKP change tack, embracing its role as a regional inspiration for the states in transition.

Current Turkish Prime Minister Ahmet Davutoglu, in the 2001 book *Strategic Depth*, set out a new theory of geopolitics and argued that the end of the Cold War had allowed Turkey to act as a 'centre state' in its own historical hinterland. Following the AKP's election to government in 2002, Ankara's foreign policy aimed to remove the artificial barriers drawn after the dismemberment of the Ottoman Empire in the wake of the First World War to reconnect Turkey with its neighbours through a concept of Muslim unity that transcended state sovereignty. The removal of these barriers, it argued, would help to facilitate the expansion of Turkish influence and to revive cultural links between Turkey and its Middle Eastern neighbours. This understanding of regional affairs was based on the belief that the era of European-inspired political and ethnic nationalism was a historical anachronism in the Middle East – destined to fail and be replaced with governments more representative of the 'Muslim masses'.

However, up until September 2011, the AKP chose to blend certain elements of this policy of strategic depth with *realpolitik*, in a policy later dubbed *ostpolitik*. This policy meant that the AKP overlooked certain elements of strategic depth and instead focused on strengthening relations with regional autocrats in politically stable countries.

Looking back, Turkey's greatest foreign-policy successes under AKP rule took place during the period of *ostpolitik* (2002–11). Ankara concluded a free-trade agreement with Syria, benefiting from close relations with its leader, Bashar Al-Assad, and lifted visa restrictions with many of its neighbours. Moreover, shortly before the start of the Arab upheavals, the AKP had begun discussions about a visa-free zone, known collectively as 'Shamgen', in many of the areas of historic Bilad Al-Sham, encompassing greater Syria, Lebanon, and extending further east to include Jordan.[1] Had these discussions come to fruition, Ankara would have been able to take a further step towards integrating areas along the Mediterranean coast and into the Levant – most of which the AKP considered to be a part of Turkey's natural hinterland.

By contrast, the AKP's ensuing foreign-policy troubles came about as a result of its decision to try to shape internal politics in states undergoing political turmoil by supporting religiously conservative political parties linked to the Muslim Brotherhood – mainly within the historic territories of Bilad Al-Sham. Ankara's support for the Muslim Brotherhood was premised on the AKP's historical links to the group, as well as on Davutoglu's embrace of the concepts of *Tawhid* (oneness with, or acceptance of, Allah) and *Tanzih* (a belief in the purity of Allah) as the two ideal sources of political legitimacy in the Muslim world.[2] In embracing these concepts, Davutoglu argued that political instability in the region was a result of the import of Western political constructs ill-suited to the Muslim world.

In this spirit, Turkey had already begun to work with the Iraqi Islamic Party (IIP – a branch of the Muslim Brotherhood) in 2005, and began to support Hamas in 2006. A later decision by the AKP to help to create the Iraqi political movement Iraqiya in 2009 ended in Ankara losing considerable influence with the Iraqi Shia political parties that maintained political control in Baghdad. Meanwhile, the AKP's support of Hamas over Fatah was a source of concern in both Jerusalem and Ramallah, and ultimately undermined Ankara's ability to act as a mediator in the Palestine–Israel and Fatah–Hamas conflicts. Indeed, after the Israeli killing of nine Turkish citizens aboard the *Mavi Marmara*, Ankara largely abandoned its relationship with Israel in favour of closer ties with Hamas.[3] This shattering of Ankara's image as a neutral mediator – a key element of its policy of *ostpolitik* – resulted in the AKP being able to talk to only one side during the frequent Hamas–Israel clashes in Gaza that followed.[4]

[1] Gokhan Kurtaran, 'Regional Free Zone Attempt Stillborn', *Hurriyet Daily News*, 1 December 2011; *Milliyet*, 'Samgen vizesinde anlasmaya varildi!', 8 March 2011.
[2] Ahmet Davutoglu, 'The Impacts of Alternative Weltanschauungs on Political Theories: A Comparison of the Tawhid and Ontological Proximity', PhD thesis, 1990, pp. 65–67.
[3] Dan Arbell, 'Turbulence in Turkey–Israel Relations Raises Doubts Over Reconciliation Process', Brookings Institution, 1 November 2013.
[4] Taha Ozhan, 'The New "Israel-US Axis"', *Middle East Eye*, 5 August 2014.

Despite these early setbacks, Turkey's position in the region was temporarily bolstered by the Arab upheavals in late 2010. Turkey initially adopted a cautious approach to the uprising in Tunisia, waiting until then-President Zine El-Abidine Ben Ali's overthrow was assured before making any official statements about the unrest. In contrast, Ankara eagerly advocated the overthrow of then-Egyptian President Hosni Mubarak just six days after the start of large-scale street protests. However, as the unrest spread to Libya, Ankara once again opted for caution, choosing to push for cosmetic political reform, rather than supporting external intervention. Turkey's caution also extended to Syria, where for much of 2011 its policy was defined by a preference for the political status quo, rather than supporting any radical changes to the country's political system.

Turkey only fully embraced political change in the Arab world in September 2011, after its months-long effort to convince Syrian leader Bashar Al-Assad to make cosmetic democratic reforms failed.[5] This prompted Ankara to completely sever its ties with the regime in Damascus and, as in other states undergoing political unrest, Turkey began to back the Muslim Brotherhood. This embrace of political change coincided with the notion of a 'Turkish model' for the states in transition in the Middle East.[6] Whilst the AKP expressed discomfort with the term, the party embraced the notion that it could act as an 'inspiration' and eagerly sought to use the likely election of Muslim Brotherhood-affiliated parties across the region to its advantage. Indeed, Ankara interpreted the political changes in the region as a reaffirmation of the arguments made by Davutoglu in *Strategic Depth*, and began to argue that the 'regional order' was undergoing a profound transformation that portended the end of the US-backed security order in the region. Some in the AKP have argued that this order – which has been referred to as both the 'US–Israel' axis[7] and the 'Camp David order'[8] – is premised on Western support for Arab autocracy and political repression. Overturning it would, in turn, upend the conditions that had allowed Arab autocrats to 'rule with an iron first' and force the region's leaderships to be more attentive to the will of their citizens.[9] This understanding of regional events prompted the AKP to

---

[5] Christopher Phillips, 'Into the Quagmire: Turkey's Frustrated Syria Policy', MENAP Briefing Paper 2012/04, Chatham House, December 2012.
[6] Kemal Kirsici, 'The Rise and Fall of Turkey as a Model for the Arab World', Brookings Institution, 15 August 2013.
[7] Ahmet Davutoglu, 'Turkiye Israil Guvenlik Anlasmasi ve Yeni Dengeler', *Yeni Safak*, 9 April 1996.
[8] Taha Ozhan, 'The Camp David Order and the United States', *Hurriyet Daily News*, 9 March 2012.
[9] Taha Ozhan, 'The Arab Spring and Turkey: The Camp David Order vs. the New Middle East', *Insight Turkey* (Vol. 13, No. 4, 2011), pp. 55–64.

disregard its previous policy of *ostpolitik* and instead promote a new vision for the region based on support for the Muslim Brotherhood – a conservative political ally that embraced a political ideology similar to the ideals of *tawhid* and *tanzih*.

Indeed, Turkey pursued this policy despite the growing anti-Brotherhood sentiment among governments in the region; the relative stability of Arab monarchies during the upheavals;[10] and the likelihood that this decision would undermine its relationships with some of the region's key actors. Regardless of these factors, Turkey pledged to 'sustain the deep and dear friendship … established with the people and to not trade these ties for temporary balance of power calculation[s]'. This approach to foreign policy and specifically to regional affairs, as articulated by Davutoglu in April 2012, suggested that Ankara would continue to support people 'who rise to demand such basic rights as freedom of expression and other political freedoms.' This policy of support for actors deemed to be oppressed is likely to continue to manifest itself through continued support for the Muslim Brotherhood, regardless of the backlash from the Arab monarchies. It would appear that Turkey has positioned itself on the side of the people, rather than, in the words of Davutoglu, the region's 'archaic regimes'.[11]

At the time the decision was made to change Turkey's policy, it seemed to the AKP that the arguments Davutoglu had put forward in his numerous writings on the geopolitics of the Middle East were on the verge of coming to fruition. Thus, it seemed that it was now in Turkey's interest to stand on the 'right side of history' and support the momentous political change in the region. This signalled the end of the pursuit of its longstanding policy of 'zero problems with neighbours' in favour of a more interventionist foreign policy, predicated on the success of a particular political party.

This shift is perhaps best symbolised by Ankara's policies in Syria. After severing ties with the Assad regime in September 2011, Ankara actively supported the Syrian political opposition and a number of different rebel groups in particular, with the aim of toppling Assad. These efforts, however, were undermined by the growing schisms within the Middle East over political Islam and the Muslim Brotherhood. On the one side, a bloc led by Saudi Arabia and the UAE resisted the empowerment of

---

[10] F Gregory Gause, 'Kings for all Seasons: How the Middle East's Monarchies Survived the Arab Spring', Brookings Doha Analysis Paper, September 2013.

[11] Ahmet Davutoglu, 'Principles of Turkish Foreign Policy and Regional Political Structuring', Vision Papers, Centre for Strategic Research, April 2012, <http://sam.gov.tr/wp-content/uploads/2012/04/vision_paper_TFP2.pdf>, accessed 14 November 2014.

the Brotherhood. On the other, Turkey and Qatar continued their efforts to support the Brotherhood throughout the region.[12]

This support incorporated Syria, where Turkey, beginning in September 2011, sought to empower the Syrian Muslim Brotherhood at the expense of other proxies favoured by the Saudi-led political bloc. Turkey's support resulted in increased infighting between the backers of the Syrian opposition and ultimately detracted from the AKP's efforts to organise a credible and organised Syrian opposition-in-exile. This resulted in Turkey and its ostensible allies in the fight against Assad supporting different rebel groups – thus helping to cripple the structures put in place to create a unified Free Syrian Army and detracting from a key element of Ankara's Syria strategy.

Moreover, in May 2014, Saudi Arabia assumed a more prominent role in organising and arming the Syrian opposition and Ankara, after coming under heavy American pressure to cease its assistance to certain rebel groups, began to take steps to bring its policies more closely into line with those of the Gulf States and the West.[13] Throughout the Syrian conflict, Ankara's support for groups like Ahrar Al-Sham and Liwa Al-Tawhid (both of which operate under the banner of the Islamic Front) was a source of controversy with its ostensible allies in the conflict: Middle Eastern states (with the exception of Qatar) and the West. Thus, the Turkish decision to back the Saudi–US-supported approach signalled Ankara's capitulation to Riyadh and Washington after years of AKP-led efforts to dictate the course of the Syrian conflict.

The symbolic end to Turkish influence in much of the Middle East came in July 2013 with the overthrow of the Egyptian Muslim Brotherhood-affiliated Freedom and Justice Party (FJP) – in which Turkey had invested substantial diplomatic capital – by the military. The demise of the FJP government of Mohamed Morsi demonstrated the continued relevance of the old regimes – which were critical in propping up the new government of Abdel Fattah Al-Sisi after the July coup – and undermined the idea that the regional order was changing. This new era of Turkish foreign policy has since been defined by the words of Ibrahim Kalin – chief policy adviser to the president – who tweeted in August 2013 that 'The claim that Turkey has been left alone in the Middle East is not true, but if it is a criticism then we should say that is a precious loneliness'.[14]

---

[12] Hassan Hassan, 'Syria Will Not Get Resolution While the Opposition Bickers', *The National*, 22 October 2014.

[13] Abdallah Suleiman Ali, 'New Alliance Could Signal End of Islamic Front', *Al-Monitor*, 4 August 2014.

[14] *Today's Zaman*, '"Zero Problems" Policy Supplanted by "Precious Loneliness" Approach', 25 August 2013.

The AKP now argues that it is following a principled foreign policy based on the decision to support democratic governance in the Middle East – itself rooted in the belief that the return to some semblance of democratic politics in the region is inevitable. In turn, Kalin's portrayal of Turkey's isolation suggests that the AKP believes that the country will eventually overcome this isolation and ultimately benefit from the soft power earned by being perceived to have stood up for Arab democracy. In contrast, the AKP has implicitly argued that the West and its Arab allies will ultimately see their influence decline, as once the region inevitably returns to electoral politics, they will be seen as having supported autocracy. Ankara therefore argues that it has adopted a long-term strategy, aimed at maintaining the soft power it achieved before – and since – the Arab upheavals.[15]

Ankara has thus continued to disregard the damage to its relationship with many Gulf States, and has instead continued to loudly condemn the July coup in Egypt.[16] The AKP has also vocally maintained its preference for the toppling of Assad in Syria and has brushed aside criticism of Turkish foreign-policy missteps, such as the AKP's handling of the Syrian conflict, its relationship with Shia political parties in Baghdad, and the judgements made about the inevitability of change to the region's political order.[17] Instead, the AKP blames the US, arguing that it was American policies in Syria, Iraq and the region more broadly that contributed to the chaos in Syria, Iraq and Egypt.

Yet these attempts to deflect criticism cannot disguise the fact that Ankara's recent decision-making has undermined the successes achieved between 2002 and 2010. Despite having established cordial relations with much of the Arab world during this period, the AKP now has poor relations with its Middle Eastern neighbours along the Mediterranean coast and throughout the Levant. Turkey's relationship with Israel is fraught with tension; Turkey recalled its ambassador to Tel Aviv in May 2010 and later expelled Israel's ambassador in September 2011 after the publication of a UN report on the *Mavi Marmara* incident.[18] In Jordan, King Abdullah has identified the AKP as part of what he has derogatorily labelled the 'Muslim Brotherhood crescent' and has publicly expressed his distrust of President Erdogan.[19] Elsewhere, in Iraqi Kurdistan, Turkey's relationship

---

[15] Jonny Hogg and Nick Tattersal, 'Turkey, Frustrated with West, Clings to Fading Vision for the Middle East', *Reuters*, 1 October 2014.
[16] *Al-Arabiya*, 'Erdogan Slams Sisi as Tyrant', 26 July 2014.
[17] Kilic Bugra Kanat, 'Turkish Foreign Policy in the New Era', *New Turkey*, 4 September 2014.
[18] *Haaretz*, 'Turkey Recalls Envoy over Gaza Flotilla Deaths, Accuses Israel of "State Terrorism"', 31 May 2010; *BBC News*, 'Turkey Expels Israeli Ambassador over Gaza Flotilla Row', 2 September 2011.
[19] Jeffrey Goldberg, 'The Modern King in the Arab Spring', *The Atlantic*, 18 March 2013.

with President Masoud Barzani remains relatively strong, but many within Iraq's Kurdistan Democratic Party (KDP) are upset by Ankara's handling of the siege of Erbil and its hands-off policy on Kobane.[20] Ankara's political proxies in Iraq – the Nujaifi brothers – have seen their influence decline as Dawa further consolidated its power in Baghdad; and Turkish-supported Sunni politicians still wield little influence over government decision-making. For example, current Iraqi Prime Minister Haider Al-Abadi's appointment of Khalid Al-Ubidy – a Sunni politician – as the minister of defence does not represent a serious break from the Maliki-era status quo, owing to the fact that the prime minister will remain the commander-in-chief of the country's armed forces.[21] Similarly, his appointment of Turkish-backed Osama Al-Nujaifi as one of two vice presidents is of little consequence with regard to Iraqi–Turkish relations, not least because Abadi's 'new' cabinet includes many hold-overs from Maliki's government, which broke with Turkey in 2010.[22] Moreover, Turkey and Iran now find themselves on opposite sides of a proxy war in Syria, leading to tensions and division, despite having taken numerous steps to bolster trade and build trust in the years before the Arab upheavals.

Nevertheless, Ankara continues to argue that its 'principled' foreign policy – which it intends to continue pursuing in the long term – will ultimately pay off.[23] It maintains that the conditions that led to the Arab upheavals remain. As such, it is held, Turkey will eventually benefit from the inevitable return of democratic politics in the Arab world, which will in turn put pressure on the Arab monarchies to undertake democratic reform.

This argument, however, is based on a revisionist interpretation of history and optimistic assessments about Ankara's image in the Middle East. To be sure, Ankara has retained support from the Muslim Brother-hood. However, Turkish policies in Syria and Iraq have resulted in the AKP being perceived, particularly by the Alevis,[24] as pursuing a sectarian

---

[20] Hevidar Ahmed, 'Senior Kurdistan Official: IS Was at Erbil's Gates; Turkey Did Not Help', Rudaw.net, 16 September 2014.

[21] Kirk Sowell, 'Iraqi Election Results Expose Dramatic Shifts in Power', *The National*, 9 June 2014.

[22] Alexander Whitcomb, 'Analysis: New Government More of the Same', Rudaw.net, 13 September 2014.

[23] Ahmet Davutoglu, 'Zero Problems in a New Era', *Foreign Policy*, 21 March 2013; Saban Kardas, 'Is Turkey's Long Game in Iraq a Success?', *Al Jazeera*, 3 September 2014; Kilic Bugra Kanat, 'Turkish Foreign Policy in the New Era', *New Turkey*, 4 September 2014.

[24] Ayla Albayrak, 'In Southern Turkey, Renewed Fears of Sectarian Strife', *Wall Street Journal*, 6 November 2013.

foreign policy,[25] concerned only with empowering certain Sunni political elements.[26] In tandem, Ankara's support for the Muslim Brotherhood has resulted in a loss of support from Arab states and political factions opposed to the group. In the future, Ankara will have to overcome these perceptions in order to deepen its appeal beyond a narrow constituency in the region.

Despite these challenges, the AKP remains undeterred. Ankara's actions suggest that Turkish policy-makers remain committed to their post-2011 foreign policy,[27] as well as to the conception of inevitable change to the regional order and the return to a more religiously conservative style of democratic governance. In turn, this means that Turkey is certain to continue to promote its preferred policies even in the face of extreme pressure from its Western allies to change them. Indeed, despite the fact that the policy remains a source of concern for many of Turkey's erstwhile allies – although not entirely at odds with the approach favoured in the West and much of the Gulf – the AKP has demonstrated the courage of its convictions. It seems clear, therefore, that the party will remain committed to its current foreign policy for the foreseeable future.

---

[25] Semih Idiz, 'The "Sunnification" of Turkish Foreign Policy', *Al-Monior*, 1 March 2013.

[26] Mohammed Noureddine, 'Turkey's Sectarian Foreign Policy May Backfire', *Al-Monitor*, 3 August 2012; Idiz, 'The "Sunnification" of Turkish Foreign Policy'.

[27] In August 2014, Recep Tayyip Erdogan won Turkey's first direct presidential election. Later that month, Erdogan tapped Davutoglu to succeed him as the country's prime minster. Hakan Fidan, a key architect of Turkish foreign policy, remains as the head of the country's National Intelligence Organization. The continuity in key decision-makers supports the idea that Ankara's foreign policy will remain consistent during the AKP's next five years in power. Moreover, according to Yasin Aktay, deputy chairman of the AKP who is also in charge of foreign affairs, '[We] do not foresee a prominent change in our party's foreign policy' following the election of Erdogan and a minor cabinet reshuffle. See Ali Unal, 'Our Foreign Policy is Based on Humanity, Not on Sectarianism', *Daily Sabah*, 1 September 2014.

About Whitehall Papers

The *Whitehall Paper* series provides in-depth studies of specific developments, issues or themes in the field of national and international defence and security. Published occasionally throughout the year, *Whitehall Papers* reflect the highest standards of original research and analysis, and are invaluable background material for specialists and policy-makers alike.

About RUSI

The Royal United Services Institute is the UK's leading independent think-tank on international defence and security. Its mission is to be an analytical research-led global forum for informing, influencing and enhancing public debate on a safer and more stable world.

Since its foundation in 1831, RUSI has relied on its members to support its activities. Annual membership subscriptions and donations are a key source of funding for the Institute; together with the revenue from publications and conferences, RUSI has sustained its political independence for over 180 years.

London | Brussels | Nairobi | Doha | Tokyo | Washington, DC